D0801363

Virginia Woolf

VIRGINIA WOOLF

Becoming a Writer

KATHERINE DALSIMER

823.91209
WOOLF

Yale University Press   New Haven and London

Glenview Public Library
1930 Glenview Road
Glenview, Illinois

Copyright © 2001 by Yale University.
All rights reserved.
This book may not be reproduced, in whole
or in part, including illustrations, in any form
(beyond that copying permitted by Sections 107 and 108
of the U.S. Copyright Law and except by reviewers
for the public press), without written permission
from the publishers.

Set in Caslon type by Tseng Information Systems, Inc.
Printed in the United States of America.

Library of Congress Cataloging-in-Publication Data
Dalsimer, Katherine, 1944–
Virginia Woolf : becoming a writer / Katherine Dalsimer.
p. cm.
Includes bibliographical references (p.) and index.
ISBN 0-300-09208-3 (alk. paper)
1. Woolf, Virginia, 1882–1941—Criticism and interpretation.
2. Women and literature—England—History—20th century.
3. Woolf, Virginia, 1882–1941—Childhood and youth.
4. Novelists, English—20th century—Biography.
5. Young women—England—Biography.   I. Title.
PR6045.072 Z583   2001
823'.912—dc21   2001003125

A catalogue record for this book is
available from the British Library.

The paper in this book meets the guidelines
for permanence and durability of the Committee
on Production Guidelines for Book Longevity of
the Council on Library Resources.

10 9 8 7 6 5 4 3 2 1

Glenview Public Library
1930 Glenview Road
Glenview, Illinois

JUL 18 2002

For Peter

Grateful acknowledgment is made to the following: The Society of Authors as the Literary Representative of the Estate of Virginia Woolf for permission to quote from the "Hyde Park Gate News," *The Voyage Out,* and *To the Lighthouse.*

The Executors of the Virginia Woolf Estate and The Random House Group Limited for permission to quote extracts from *A Passionate Apprentice,* originally published by Hogarth Press.

The Random House Group Ltd. for permission to quote extracts from *Moments of Being* by Virginia Woolf, edited by Jeanne Schulkind, *The Diaries of Virginia Woolf,* edited by Anne Olivier Bell, *The Letters of Virginia Woolf,* edited by Nigel Nicolson and Joanna Traumann, and *The Essays of Virginia Woolf,* edited by Andrew McNeillie, published by the Hogarth Press.

Harcourt, Inc. for permission to quote extracts from *The Voyage Out,* copyright 1920 by Harcourt, Inc. and renewed 1948 by Leonard Woolf; *To the Lighthouse,* copyright 1927 by Harcourt, Inc. and renewed 1954 by Leonard Woolf; *Moments of Being,* copyright 1976 by Quentin Bell and Angelica Garnett; *A Passionate Apprentice,* copyright 1980 by Quentin Bell and Angelica Garnett; *The Diary of Virginia Woolf,* Volume 2, copyright 1978, and Volume 3, copyright 1980, by Quentin Bell and Angelica Garnett; *The Letters of Virginia Woolf,* Volume 1, copyright 1975, and Volume 4, copyright 1978, by Quentin Bell and Angelica Garnett; *The Essays of Virginia Woolf,* Volume 1, copyright 1986, and Volume 4, copyright 1989, by Quentin Bell and Angelica Garnett.

Contents

Acknowledgments

I wish to thank Sally Brown, Curator of Modern Literary Manuscripts at the British Library for her gracious help in allowing me access to the "Hyde Park Gate News," and Rodney Phillips, Stephen Crook, and Philip Milito at the Berg Collection of the New York Public Library for their kind assistance in relation to Woolf's early diaries and drafts of *The Voyage Out*.

I benefited from discussions of this work in presentations to the Gardiner Seminar on Psychoanalysis and the Humanities at Yale, the American Psychoanalytic Association, and the Yale University Mental Health Service. An earlier version of chapter 2 appeared in *The Psychoanalytic Study of the Child*. For all that I have learned in teaching them, I thank my students at Columbia College and my supervisees at the Columbia University Mental Health Service and at the Weill Medical College of Cornell University.

My association with Yale University Press began with my previous book, and I am delighted to return to old friends. I am grateful to Gladys Topkis, who launched this book; to Susan Arellano, who has seen it through to completion; and to Lawrence Kenney, whose discerning suggestions made my manuscript a better book. I am indebted to Dr. Ruth Shapiro for her thoughtful reading of an earlier draft.

And my deepest gratitude to my family, Emily Liebert, Maggie Pouncey, Chris Pouncey, and my husband, Peter Pouncey, for their generosity to me in every way.

INTRODUCTION

This is not a biography of Virginia Woolf.

There are already many excellent ones from the last quarter of the past century,[1] and they have been buttressed by fine editions of Woolf's writings. In addition to her novels and short fiction, there are the essays and book reviews that began to appear in print when she was a young woman, and the many volumes of her diaries and letters. Unquestionably the most vibrant portrait of Virginia Woolf as a person is the one she wrote herself, over the course of a lifetime, in these diaries and letters. Their richness and abundance allow the reader, decades later, to feel the rhythms of her daily life, still to hear the cadence of her voice. Even after the telephone came into use, Woolf continued to write letters not only to tell what she was doing and thinking and to gossip, but to make the ordinary arrangements of life— to suggest what train a friend should take in order to arrive in time for tea. Many years after her death, we can know, it seems, the large and small events of Woolf's life in a given week, and, more than that, what she thought about these happenings at the time, and again later. Moreover, the generous annotation—of the letters by Nigel Nicholson and Joanna Trautman (1975-80), the diaries by Anne Olivier Bell (1977-84), the early journals by Mitchell Leaska (1990)—brings her life into focus for the contemporary reader with arresting sharpness of detail. If Woolf

1. See especially those of Bell (1972), Rose (1978), Gordon (1984), and Lee (1996).

makes a casual reference in her diary to a chamber music concert she attended the previous evening, the editor will have reclaimed the program and recorded in a footnote the very quartets Woolf heard.[2]

The documentation for Woolf's early life is less abundant, as one would expect, but even here there are surprising and sometimes delightful stores of information. Fortunately preserved, there is the family newspaper that Virginia collaborated on with her sister, Vanessa, and her brothers, Thoby and Adrian, beginning when Virginia was nine years old. Appearing under the banner "Hyde Park Gate News," it shows, along with a child's high spirits, her wit, acerbity, and sharp eye for the particular, already precociously developed. Also extant are the journals she kept at the ages of fifteen and seventeen and twenty-one, and letters from this period as well. And there are autobiographical writings. In writing one narrative of her earlier life, she was herself a young woman whose adult life had yet to shape itself; in another, she was a mature woman, looking back toward the end of her life on those earlier years, now from a very different vantage point.

My purpose in this book is to draw together this wealth of material in order to bring into sharper focus a particular time in Virginia Woolf's life. I am interested in the period when she was becoming a writer, the years of her adolescence and young womanhood. During these years, life repeatedly inflicted what she would later call "sledge-hammer blows." The first was the death of her mother when Virginia was thirteen years old. She had her first breakdown at this time, and she was thought to be still recovering when she began the earliest of the diaries I shall discuss, the journal she kept at fifteen. Over the course

2. Anne Olivier Bell (1990) describes the prodigious scholarship and detective work that went into the gathering of this information.

of the year documented in that journal, there would be another death in the family, that of her older half-sister, Stella, who after the death of their mother had stepped into the place of woman of the house. Virginia was twenty-two years old when her father, too, died; in the wake of his death she had her second breakdown. Still another death would follow two years later, that of her brother Thoby, when Virginia was twenty-four and he twenty-six, returning from a holiday in Greece. These blows fell on an individual who, as her family history suggests, had inherited a marked vulnerability; for much of her life she suffered from manic-depressive illness. Ultimately she committed suicide, walking into the River Ouse with stones in her pockets in 1941 at the age of fifty-nine.

Yet Virginia Woolf lived a life of vibrance and intensity and accomplishment in spite of the hover of illness and in spite of life's cruelty to her. My interest is in exploring the ways that writing served her. Astonishingly gifted from the start, she would grow as a writer, to become most attuned and attentive to the movements of her own mind, its shifts of light and dark, and able to catch them in the precise phrase or image that deliver them alive to the reader. In what follows we would do well, then, to let Woolf speak for herself.

She wrote in her diary on November 28, 1928, "I will read Proust, I think; I will go backwards & forwards." It is not only Proust who does this; it is what we *all* do when we use memory and reflection to make sense of our lives. And it is what we do in the clinical situation, observing the flow of thought, fantasy, feeling, memory and, carried along by it, moving between present and past. In what follows we shall keep company with Virginia Woolf as she moves backward and forward over an earlier period of her life, from different ages, perspectives, and vantage points, reading the work of her maturity as well as her early writings.

I start with her great novel *To the Lighthouse,* which, as her diaries and letters record, she intended to be autobiographical. In the memoir she wrote toward the end of her life, she looked back not only upon the childhood events and the dramatis personae that were the fictional substance of the novel; she reflected also upon the *writing* of the novel, and the ways that writing *To the Lighthouse* altered her relationship with her parents who had died many years earlier.

The various tellings of her life, from various points in the course of her life, confirm for readers what Woolf herself knew well: memory tells a changing story. Inevitably the climate of one's present mental landscape alters the past. But the yellowing pages of the "Hyde Park Gate News" preserve the children's view of their family life in the present tense—as it unfolded, week by week. After discussing the newspaper that the children collaborated on, I turn to Virginia's early journals and letters and to her first efforts as a writer. Drawing together the various strands, we have, it seems, "life and the memory of it." Elizabeth Bishop's phrase, from the poem she called "Poem," makes a careful distinction between the two.

The earliest of Woolf's writings to appear in print were book reviews and essays, which she published regularly from the age of twenty-two. Most were unsigned, but her own voice can be heard in them—and the first sounding of themes that she would develop through the work of her maturity. Letters from this time express her nervousness and self-doubt; but the pieces themselves are often highly accomplished, assured in tone. These reviews and essays mark the beginning of Woolf's career as a writer. I turn from them to consider at some length her first novel. Begun when she was twenty-five, *The Voyage Out* was published eight years later after much revision. Though flawed as fiction and certainly the least read of her novels, it is nonetheless revealing of Woolf herself as a young woman, especially when read in the light of the earlier drafts that she chose to exclude from the novel she published.

I conclude with a chapter "On Being Ill," its title borrowed from an essay Woolf wrote at a time when she intended to begin writing *To the Lighthouse* but was prevented from doing so by one of her periodic breakdowns. Her essay provides a point of entry into the subject of Woolf's complex and contradictory relation with the illness that haunted her for much of her life. Was her illness a terrible, wasteful obstacle to her creativity—or the necessary condition for it? No one has posed the question more compellingly, or more disturbingly.

Woolf's writings invite one to examine the way a life is told and retold over the course of time, by a writer who was herself intensely interested in the working of memory. Why, she asked, do I remember some things so vividly and others, seemingly, not at all? How is it that memory may ignore whole passages of one's life and then seize upon a particular event or image or moment and hold it in the most searching light? Woolf examines such moments tirelessly; she does not let her mind settle on a final judgment of the pictures memory has offered her but is continually studying them again and reading them differently at different times. Perhaps the experience of early loss makes memory itself a matter of urgent concern. It is memory that maintains our living connection with the dead; it is the most palpable way to preserve what is otherwise irrevocably lost.

"Scene-making," Woolf observed, "is my natural way of marking the past." She was referring to her proclivities as a writer. But scene making as a way of marking the past is not reserved to the novelist; it is what we all do. Memory selects from the continuous flow of life particular scenes that serve not simply as a record of the past: indeed, as Woolf suggests, these remembered scenes may be constructed. Her felicitous phrase captures a notion with a long and complex history in the psychoanalytic literature. In his paper "Screen Memories" (1899) Freud raised the question of why particular scenes from childhood appear to be fixed in memory, and proposed that childhood "memories" may be made, or constructed, in ways that are outside awareness. As he put it, a fantasy that remains unconscious "must be content to find its way allusively . . . into a childhood scene" (p. 317). It is the "allusiveness" of remembered scenes that is germane to my reading of Woolf's writings.

I am a clinical psychologist. In doing clinical work the therapist learns to be especially attentive to such scenes. In a patient's narrative, the force of feeling is always conveyed most tellingly *in the particular:* the incident, the gesture, the image. Scene making is the way we all mark the past, and the scenes the writer creates, like the scenes that memory shapes, are the bearers of meaning. Whether selected or constructed—most often both—these scenes have the evocative power of metaphor, compressing into a singular image whole worlds of experience and feeling and fantasy, conscious and unconscious.

For this reason I have found, in teaching and in supervising the work of beginning psychologists and psychiatrists, that the close reading of literary texts is excellent "ear training" for the kind of listening that the clinical situation requires. It opens to the attentive listener a complex counterpoint between the patient's narrative, both verbal and nonverbal, and the therapist's own emotional responses.

To move backward and forward in time is the familiar rhythm of clinical work: we examine the present in the light of the remembered past, and that past in the light of the present. But in reading the early writings of Virginia Woolf we know not only her past; we also know her future. We read the journals she kept at ages fifteen, seventeen, and twenty-one, the book reviews and essays she wrote in her twenties, her early fiction, the letters she wrote as she began to publish her work—we read these knowing the writer she would become, the life she would live, and ultimately the death she would choose.

In spite of her terrible darknesses, Woolf had a capacity to be vibrantly engaged with the world around her—the simple pleasures of the day as well as the great human moments and human absurdities. The quotidian rhythms of life gave her deep satisfaction. She relished the excitement of walking through London streets and the peacefulness of long afternoon walks through the Sussex countryside. Always, at the center of it all, the very heart of the matter, was her writing.

This is my subject. I wish to explore the ways that writing served Virginia Woolf in the period when she was becoming a writer, the ways it served her in the face of the "sledge-hammer blows" that life dealt. From an early age, writing was as necessary to her as the very air she breathed: before finishing one book she began to envisage the next, to ensure that there would be no time when she was not working. It was writing that consoled and sustained her—as much as it was possible for her to be consoled or sustained.

I

To the Lighthouse

"We think back through our mothers if we are women," Virginia Woolf declared in *A Room of One's Own*. Her observation is one that lodges in the imagination and takes root there, deepening through time. Woolf was referring to literary tradition. Where, she asked, could Jane Austen, Charlotte Brontë, George Eliot turn for precedent as they set pen to paper? What tradition did the great women novelists of the nineteenth century have to draw upon? But her metaphor reaches further and deeper than questions of literary antecedents. In the years since she wrote those words, Virginia Woolf herself has become one of those "mothers" we think back through. And in the work that many consider her finest, the novel *To the Lighthouse*, she has given readers another in the fictional character of Mrs. Ramsay.

What I wish to do in this chapter is to think back through Mrs. Ramsay, a mother who is a creation of the imagination, to Virginia Woolf herself and to her own mother. Toward the end of her life, looking back, she stated that in writing *To the Lighthouse* she had "ceased to be obsessed" by her mother, who had died many years earlier. I want to consider the relationship of a daughter who is a grown woman with the mother who died when she was a girl—in Woolf's own words, with the "invisible presence" of her mother. Centering my discussion on the novel, I shall also draw upon Woolf's memoirs, diaries and letters, and an essay. Taken together, they allow one to explore the relationship of Virginia Woolf in her maturity with a mother long dead—and the ways in which the writing of her autobiographical novel both reflected and revised that internal relationship.

Her diaries and letters make clear that Woolf intended *To the Lighthouse* to be autobiographical, a portrait in fiction of her parents and of childhood summers at St. Ives in Cornwall. What makes her memoir especially rich in relation to my concerns is that she looks back not only to her early years and to the family life she represented fictionally in *To the Lighthouse*, but also to the writing of the novel—and the profound impact it had upon her.

Here is her account:

> Until I was in the 40's . . . the presence of my mother obsessed me. I could hear her voice, see her, imagine what she would do or say as I went about my day's doings. She was one of the invisible presences who after all play so important a part in every life. . . . she obsessed me, in spite of the fact that she died when I was thirteen, until I was forty-four. Then one day I made up, as I sometimes make up my books, *To the Lighthouse;* in a great, apparently involuntary, rush. One thing burst into another. Blowing bubbles out of a pipe gives the feeling of the rapid crowd of ideas and scenes which blew out of my mind, so that my lips seemed syllabling of their own accord as I walked. What blew the bubbles? Why then? I have no notion. But I wrote the book very quickly; and when it was written, I ceased to be obsessed by my mother. I no longer hear her voice; I do not see her. ("A Sketch of the Past," 80–81)

How did the writing of the book have this impact? Here Woolf's language subsides, most uncharacteristically, into banality, and slides past the very question one wants to see engaged. She continues, "I suppose that I did for myself what psychoanalysts do for their patients. I expressed some very long felt and deeply felt emotion. And in expressing it I explained it and then laid it to rest."

To my mind, this passage raises more questions than it answers. To say that she "expressed" a deeply felt emotion does not in itself account for the magnitude of the effect. How does expressing it constitute an explanation? Why should an explanation lay the feeling to rest? And what, precisely, *is* laid to rest? I should like to press the matter further. For much of her life her mother, long dead, was a constant "invisible presence"; after writing *To the Lighthouse* Woolf no longer felt haunted by her. Why?

Virginia Woolf was born in 1882 into a large and very interesting family—born, as she wrote, "not of rich parents, but of well-to-do parents, born into a very communicative, literate, letter-writing, articulate late 19th century world." Her father, Sir Leslie Stephen, was an eminent Victorian man of letters, author of *A History of English Thought in the Eighteenth Century, The Science of Ethics,* and *Social Rights and Duties,* among many books, and editor of the *Dictionary of National Biography.* Her mother, Julia Duckworth Stephen, was considered by her contemporaries an exceptionally beautiful woman and still seems so today in the well-known portrait of her by her aunt, the photographer Julia Margaret Cameron. The relatives and friends of the large extended family included many leading figures of the intellectual, literary, and artistic worlds of the late Victorian era.

Both of Virginia Woolf's parents had been married previously, and both had been widowed. Leslie Stephen's first wife, Minny Thackeray, was a daughter of the novelist. When she died, he was left with a five-year-old daughter, Laura, who was considered mentally deficient. Julia Stephen's previous marriage was to a barrister, Herbert Duckworth. When he died, she was left with two young children, George and Stella, and a third, Gerald, was born six weeks after the death of his father. Julia Duckworth was a widow at twenty-four and remained a widow for eight years. As a close friend of the Thackeray sisters, she knew Leslie Stephen and was a sympathetic friend to him in his bereavement. Two and a half years after the death of his first wife, Leslie Stephen and Julia Duckworth were married. He was forty-six and she was thirty-two.

There were four children born of this marriage within four and a half years: Vanessa, born on May 30, 1879; Thoby, on September 8, 1880; Virginia, on January 25, 1882; and Adrian, on October 27, 1883. Thus there were eight children altogether, including the half-sisters and half-brothers, and in addition there were always relatives and visitors. Julia Stephen, besides managing this crowded and complicated household, took on other responsibilities, visiting the needy and the sick. Woolf conveyed the press of competing demands upon her mother in a description of the contents of Julia's desk on the day she died. In that morning's mail "there was a letter from a woman whose daughter had been betrayed and [who] asked for help; a letter from George, from Aunt Mary, from a nurse who was out of work, some bills, some begging letters, and many sheets from a girl who had quarrelled with her parents and must reveal her soul" ("Reminiscences," 38). Julia's husband was a difficult, demanding man; there were eight children, of different ages, with different needs. The household was large; and moreover there were the strangers to whom she gave her care. Years later her daughter would reach back in memory toward her mother and find little to hold onto: "Can I remember ever being alone with her for more than a few minutes? Someone was always interrupting. When I think of her spontaneously she is always in a room full of people

. . . What a jumble of things I can remember, if I let my mind run, about my mother; but they are all of her in company; of her surrounded; of her generalised; dispersed" ("A Sketch of the Past," 83–84).

Woolf's earliest memory of her mother, she wrote, was "of her lap; the scratch of some beads on her dress comes back to me as I pressed my cheek against it." This sense memory that "comes back" to her, whose importance she underscores by designating it her earliest memory, compresses into a single moment a poignant theme that threads itself through these memoirs. Beads on a mother's dress seem glittering and glamorous to a young girl—but are best admired from a distance.

Woolf does describe a moment of having her mother's full attention. Significantly, she won it with her writing: "How excited I used to be when the 'Hyde Park Gate News' was laid on her plate on Monday morning, and she liked something I had written! Never shall I forget my extremity of pleasure—it was like being a violin and being played upon—when I found that she had sent a story of mine to Madge Symonds; it was so imaginative, she said." For four years the "Hyde Park Gate News" appeared weekly, with news of the Stephen family often humorously embroidered by the young Virginia. This chronicle stopped abruptly when her mother died.

The death of Julia Stephen, who died of rheumatic fever after an eight-week illness, was shattering. Soon afterward, Virginia had her first breakdown. She became painfully excitable and nervous, then severely depressed and morbidly self-critical, blaming herself for being vain and egotistical. She was intensely irritable, "terrified of people, blushed scarlet if spoke to and was unable to face a stranger in the street" (Bell 1972, 45). She heard for the first time then what she was later to call "those horrible voices." She would hear them for the last time in the weeks before her death: "It is just as it was the first time. . . . I have fought against it, but I cant any longer," she wrote in her suicide note to her sister.

The death of her mother, devastating in itself, was not all that Virginia suffered at this time: with the death of his wife, Leslie Stephen went into a period of pathological mourning, punctuated by bellowings of grief. It was a time Woolf would describe as "a period of Oriental gloom, for surely there was something in the darkened rooms, the groans, the passionate lamentations that passed the normal limits of sorrow, and hung about the genuine tragedy with folds of Eastern drapery" ("Reminiscences," 40). As he yielded to self-dramatizing self-pity, the children who had themselves lost their mother were enlisted to comfort their bereaved father. Looking back many years later, Woolf wrote, "The tragedy of her death was not that it made one, now and then and very intensely, unhappy. It was that it made her unreal; and us solemn, and self-conscious. We were made to act parts that we did not feel; to fumble for words that we did not know. It obscured, it dulled. It made one hypocritical and immeshed in the conventions of sorrow" ("A Sketch of the Past," 95).

The death of her mother was the first in a series of losses.[1] Virginia Woolf was early acquainted with grief—and grief is, I think, at the heart of her autobiographical novel.

This sketch of the Stephen family—a beautiful wife and mother, an intellectual husband, eight children, a household

1. There is a rich psychoanalytic literature on early loss which informs all that follows. See especially Loewald (1962), Jacobson (1965), Wolfenstein (1966, 1969), Siggins (1966), Furman (1974), Bowlby (1961, 1980). There is a rich literature, too, on the relation between mourning and creativity. See especially Pollock (1961, 1989), Hamilton (1969), Liebert (1983).

crowded with guests, summers at the sea, all brought to an end by the death of the mother—will seem familiar to readers of *To the Lighthouse*. And an entry in her diary, written as she conceived the novel, makes the connection explicit. Here is what she envisioned: "This is going to be fairly short: to have father's character done complete in it; & mothers; & St. Ives; & childhood; & all the usual things I try to put in—life, death, &c. But the centre is father's character, sitting in a boat, reciting We perished, each alone, while he crushes a dying mackerel" (*Diary* 3:18-19). This plan must seem surprising to readers of the novel, for its center is unquestionably not father's character, but mother's. It is she who exerts a hold over the imaginations of the other characters; it is she about whom their thoughts circle again and again without coming to rest. We see her through the eyes, the thoughts, the memories of each of the characters by turns. In the words of one of those characters, "Fifty pairs of eyes were not enough to get round that one woman with." The movement of the narrative, with its continually shifting point of view, may itself be seen as an effort to "get round" Mrs. Ramsay, if not with fifty pairs of eyes, then with more than any one person can possess. In writing *To the Lighthouse* Woolf was "thinking back through" Mrs. Ramsay to her own mother, and it is for this reason that this fictional presence came to command the center of the imaginative world of the novel—for the other characters, for readers and critics, and for Woolf herself—regardless of her conscious intention when she began to write.

In the first part of the novel, quite near the beginning, there is an explicit image of a girl who is grieving, but it is very easy to read past. It is hidden within the folds of a long, convoluted sentence:

> Disappearing as stealthily as stags from the dinner-table directly the meal was over, the eight sons and

daughters of Mr. and Mrs. Ramsay sought their
bedrooms, their fastnesses in a house where there
was no other privacy to debate anything, everything; Tansley's tie; the passing of the Reform Bill;
sea birds and butterflies; people; while the sun
poured into those attics, which a plank alone separated from each other so that every footstep could
be plainly heard and the Swiss girl sobbing for her
father who was dying of cancer in a valley of the
Grisons, and lit up bats, flannels, straw hats, ink-
pots, beetles, and the skulls of small birds, while it
drew from the long frilled strips of seaweed pinned
to the wall a smell of salt and weeds, which was
in the towels too, gritty with sand from bathing.
(16–17)

The sobbing girl is alluded to in the second part of a subordinate clause within a subordinate clause; the complex syntax of the sentence requires that the reader connect a subject ("the sun") with a verb ("lit up") that is located fully four lines later, so that the reader is forced to move quickly past what intervenes, the sobbing girl, in order to make sense of the sentence. When the verb finally appears, it is immediately followed by a list, an item-ization of the clutter of an attic, so that the sobbing of the girl becomes merely an item of that clutter—both of the attic, and of the sentence. Amid this clutter, the sobs of the girl are given equal weight with the sound of passing footsteps: everything in the structure of the sentence contrives to muffle her sobs, to silence her grief. The fierce submersion of grief, enacted briefly here, is central to this text.

The opening line of the novel is Mrs. Ramsay's; hers is the first voice we hear:

"Yes, of course, if it's fine tomorrow," said Mrs. Ramsay. "But you'll have to be up with the lark," she added.

To her son these words conveyed an extraordinary joy, as if it were settled, the expedition were bound to take place, and the wonder to which he had looked forward, for years and years it seemed, was, after a night's darkness and a day's sail, within touch. Since he belonged, even at the age of six, to that great clan which cannot keep this feeling separate from that, but must let future prospects, with their joys and sorrows, cloud what is actually at hand, since to such people even in earliest childhood any turn in the wheel of sensation has the power to crystallise and transfix the moment upon which its gloom or radiance rests, James Ramsay, sitting on the floor cutting out pictures from the illustrated catalogue of the Army and Navy Stores, endowed the picture of a refrigerator, as his mother spoke, with heavenly bliss. It was fringed with joy. (9)

What Woolf conveys here is not simply the point of view of a young child, but a child's mode of experience. James is given to great sweeps of feeling, and whatever the mood of the present moment, it takes over the whole of his emotional life. The hedges, the qualifications of adult thought (his mother's "if") disappear: it is settled, the expedition is certain to take place. The categories of adult thought are not yet in place; past, present, and future swirl into one another and are indistinguishable. The joy that James anticipates in the future expedition suffuses the present with its radiance. And it suffuses the present in the particular, in the concrete details of his activity. There is an immediacy to his sense impressions: one must be small in stature to hear, as James does, the knocking of brooms, the rustling of dresses. This is where Woolf places the reader at the very outset. It is significant that Mr. and Mrs. Ramsay, unlike the other characters, are not given first names. The reader is positioned to look up at them, as a child would.

Mrs. Ramsay's "yes" has the power to fill her son's whole being with joy. And then Mr. Ramsay appears:

> "But," said his father, stopping in front of the drawing-room window, "it won't be fine."
>
> Had there been an axe handy, or a poker, any weapon that would have gashed a hole in his father's breast and killed him, there and then, James would have seized it. Such were the extremes of emotion that Mr. Ramsay excited in his children's breasts by his mere presence; standing, as now, lean as a knife, narrow as the blade of one, grinning sarcastically, not only with the pleasure of disillusioning his son and casting ridicule upon his wife, who was ten thousand times better in every way than he was (James thought), but also with some secret conceit at his own accuracy of judgment. What he said was true. It was always true. (10)

Mrs. Ramsay's single word "yes" opens the gates of heaven. Mr. Ramsay's single word "but" slams them shut. His "but" is a word of dispute and obstruction. He is an academic, a philosopher: he does his spoiling of pleasure in a way that gathers about itself a cloak of unassailability, the claim of truth.

Mr. Ramsay is the personification of Victorian patriarchal culture, and he bears the whole weight of that culture. He is a philosopher of some stature: the extent of his achievement, the measure of that stature, is his endless preoccupation. Was his last book quite his best?

> For if thought is like the keyboard of a piano, di-
> vided into so many notes, or like the alphabet is
> ranged in twenty-six letters all in order, then his
> splendid mind had no sort of difficulty in running
> over those letters one by one, firmly and accurately,
> until it had reached, say, the letter Q. He reached
> Q. Very few people in the whole of England ever
> reach Q. . . . But after Q? What comes next? After
> Q there are a number of letters the last of which is
> scarcely visible to mortal eyes, but glimmers red in
> the distance. Z is only reached once by one man in
> a generation. Still, if he could reach R it would be
> something. (53–54)

If Mr. Ramsay's intellectual range extends to Q, his emotional range is much narrower. Vain, self-absorbed, demanding, childish, needy, Mr. Ramsay is not interesting enough to hold the center of the book. He announces his character complete in his first word. It is the mother who fascinates and eludes.

In the opening scene of *To the Lighthouse*, Mrs. Ramsay is framed in the window of the house with her son James at her knee. We glimpse the intimacy of the mother watching him in his private world and enjoying him. While the young boy is absorbed in cutting out pictures, she is knitting. After her husband has dashed the boy's hopes and aroused his hatred by predicting that the weather will not be fine, that the expedition to the lighthouse will not take place, Mrs. Ramsay tries to soothe James's feelings: "But it may be fine—I expect it will be fine." Her only expression of irritation with her husband is an impatient twist of the stocking she is knitting, to be brought to the lighthouse keeper for his son. She will bring, too, some old magazines to help alleviate the boredom of the watch. In a passage vividly imagined, she conjures up the dreariness and loneliness of the lighthouse keeper's life, the worry he must have about the wife and children from whom he is obliged to live apart. In the opening pages of *To the Lighthouse*, Mrs. Ramsay places herself in that female tradition in which taking care of others—family, visitors, even strangers—constitutes one's lifework.

Mrs. Ramsay is a beautiful woman, even now. She is a woman men fall in love with, and she has this power still. Her husband's priggish student, Charles Tansley (whose dissertation, Mrs. Ramsey recalls, was about the influence of something upon somebody), walking into town with her, cannot help himself:

> With stars in her eyes and veils in her hair, with cyclamen and wild violets—what nonsense was he thinking? She was fifty at least; she had eight children. Stepping through fields of flowers and taking to her breast buds that had broken and lambs that had fallen; with the stars in her eyes and the wind in her hair—He took her bag.
>
> . . . and they walked up the street, she holding her parasol erect and walking as if she expected to meet someone round the corner, while for the first time in his life Charles Tansley felt an extraordinary pride; a man digging in a drain stopped digging and looked at her, let his arm fall down and looked at her; for the first time in his life Charles Tansley felt an extraordinary pride; felt the wind and the cyclamen and the violets for he was walking with a beautiful woman. He had hold of her bag. (25)

The student Charles Tansley; the botanist William Bankes, who feels a sort of "rapture," even "worship," in her presence; Mr. Ramsay himself, who could not help noticing, as he passed, the sternness of her beauty; the poets who have inscribed their volumes to her; the young Paul Rayley, who asks Minta Doyle to marry him because of Mrs. Ramsay—the novel is filled with men who are in one way or another in love with Mrs. Ramsay, who feel her extraordinary power.

But it is not only men who feel this power. The painter Lily Briscoe gropes in her mind for the words that would describe accurately her feeling for Mrs. Ramsay. She "had much ado to control her impulse to fling herself (thank Heaven she had always resisted so far) at Mrs. Ramsay's knee and say to her—but what could one say to her?—'I'm in love with you'? No, that was not true. 'I'm in love with this all,' waving her hand at the hedge, at the house, at the children. It was absurd, it was impossible" (32–33). Lily is in love with Mrs. Ramsay in spite of herself. And I believe that Virginia Woolf is too, in spite of her efforts not to be.

There is surely evidence in the text that what Woolf meant to do was to hold the Ramsays up to feminist scrutiny. She wants the reader to see that their rigid division of the world into male and female, masculine and feminine, is fatal. In the generation that follows theirs, it all comes to its inevitable conclusion, with a son and a daughter dying symbolic deaths—dying, one might say, of their genders. Andrew, the brightest and most promising of the sons, the one Mr. Ramsay thought would be a better man than he had been, will die in the Great War. Prue, the daughter Mrs. Ramsay expected would turn out to be more beautiful than she herself had been, the one whose beauty took one's breath away, will die in childbirth. Woolf means us to see the mortal consequences of the division into masculine and feminine, of the polarity between the sexes.

Mrs. Ramsay is the Victorian ideal of a woman, the Angel in the House, spending her soul looking after the needs of others: of her young son, for whom she must find an intricate picture to cut out, a rake perhaps, to distract him from the hurt her husband has inflicted; of her husband, whose need to protect her she perceives and indulges; of her daughters, whom she allows to choose her necklace, knowing that they relish the choosing; of the lighthouse keeper and his son; of Charles Tansley, whom she defends from the barbs of the children; even of old Mr. Carmichael ("Is there anything you need from town?"). Mrs. Ramsay herself has no time to read—even those books that have been inscribed to her by the poets themselves ("To her whose wishes must be obeyed," "To the happier Helen of our days"). Mrs. Ramsay, we are repeatedly told, is shortsighted.

Both Mr. and Mrs. Ramsay stand as allegorical figures. The difference between them, though, is that Mr. Ramsay retains throughout the novel the woodenness, the abstractness of an allegorical figure, wearing his significance on his sleeve. Mrs. Ramsay is a more complex figure. She resists the constraints of allegory: in the contradictions of the author's relationship to her, Mrs. Ramsay becomes fully and unforgettably an individual.

In the character of Lily Briscoe, an artist and an incipient feminist, Woolf personifies a set of choices antithetical to those represented by Mrs. Ramsay. Lily Briscoe is aware of the temptation to do as Mrs. Ramsay does, to soothe the feelings of men, and she makes a deliberate effort to resist the temptation. Sitting opposite Charles Tansley at the dinner table,

> could she not see, as in an X-ray photograph, the ribs and thigh bones of the young man's desire to impress himself, lying dark in the mist of his flesh—that thin mist which convention had laid over his burning desire to break into the conversation? But, she thought, screwing up her Chinese eyes, and remembering how he sneered at women, 'can't paint, can't write,' why should I help him to relieve himself?
>
> There is a code of behaviour, she knew, whose

seventh article (it may be) says that on occasions of this sort it behooves the woman, whatever her own occupation may be, to go to the help of the young man opposite so that he may expose and relieve the thigh bones, the ribs, of his vanity, of his urgent desire to assert himself; as indeed it is their duty, she reflected, in her old maidenly fairness, to help us, suppose the Tube were to burst into flames. Then, she thought, I should certainly expect Mr. Tansley to get me out. But how would it be, she thought, if neither of us did either of these things? (137)

At times, not to do these things seems to Lily Briscoe an achievement, and at other times it seems her own inadequacy. Woolf keeps the reader in a similar disequilibrium, giving Lily an astute line of thought, then undercutting it with the pejorative "old maidenly." It is important, given the shifts in point of view that are the hallmark of this novel, that the phrase is not, here, the thought of Mrs. Ramsay but is spoken in the voice of the narrator—with the authority of the narrator.

At the end of the novel Lily Briscoe is forty-four years old, the age of Virginia Woolf herself when she began *To the Lighthouse*. Lily is an artist, and, like the author, she is childless. Woolf invites us to see the painter as a self-portrait, ascribing to Lily Briscoe work very like the work in which she appears as a fictional character. Lily is engaged in painting the scene that is also Woolf's subject: the mother and child framed in the window. Her painting, like the novel, is divided into three parts. And the final stroke of Lily's painting, the drawing of a line, is the final line of the novel.

The completion of Lily's painting, the final line of the novel, would seem to be presented as her triumph. But is it? Or is the reader not left wondering, like Lily, whether her work will be rolled up in attics, hung in servants' bedrooms? Lily herself cannot come to rest in her own appraisal of her art:

> What does it all mean? How do you explain it all?
> she wanted to say, turning to Mr. Carmichael. . . .
> She looked at her picture. That would have been his
> answer, presumably—how "you" and "I" and "she"
> pass and vanish; nothing stays; all changes; but not
> words, not paint. Yet it would be hung in attics, she
> thought; it would be rolled up and flung under a
> sofa; yet even so, even of a picture like that, it was
> true. One might say, even of this scrawl, not of that
> actual picture, perhaps, but of what is attempted,
> that it "remained for ever," she was going to say, or,
> for the words spoken sounded even to herself, too
> boastful, to hint, wordlessly. (267)

The fits and starts of the prose here have the rhythm of Lily's ambivalence. The clear arc of an unencumbered sentence is impossible. The contradictions in her own assessment of her art—"yet," "yet," "but"—finally are so paralyzing that even words spoken are too forceful an assertion, and her thought must be reduced to a wordless hint.

At the end of the novel, when Lily draws her line and completes her painting, her act is described in language that is pale and wan. How much more vivid, how much more convincingly imagined, is the dinner party that Mrs. Ramsay orchestrates. As the evening darkens and candles are lit, she draws the guests around the table, one by one, into the murmur of conversation. The huge brown pot has just been set before Mrs. Ramsay, and Paul Rayley, whom she has seated next to her, explains his and Minta Doyle's lateness in returning from their walk to the beach: "We went back to look for Minta's brooch." Mrs. Ramsay immediately understands that he has asked the girl to marry him, as she had hoped he would:

> "We"—that was enough. She knew from the effort, the rise in his voice to surmount a difficult word that it was the first time he had said "we." "We did this, we did that." They'll say that all their lives, she thought, and an exquisite scent of olives and oil and juice rose from the great brown dish as Marthe, with a little flourish, took the cover off. The cook had spent three days over that dish. And she must take great care, Mrs. Ramsay thought, diving into the soft mass, to choose a specially tender piece for William Bankes. And she peered into the dish, with its shiny walls and its confusion of savoury brown and yellow meats and its bay leaves and its wine, and thought, this will celebrate the occasion— (150–51)

As readers we are drawn to peer into the pot, to see its colors, to inhale the exquisite scent. The *boeuf en daube* is far more fully realized artistically than is Lily's painting, which is never made vivid, indeed is hardly made clear, and has puzzled critics.

As I said, we are never told the first name of Mrs. Ramsay, nor that of Mr. Ramsay: the reader is positioned to look up at them, as a child would. The painter, however, is often referred to by her first name only, as if she were a child. She is given a virginal name, the name of a woman who sees herself, indeed, as "not made for that": "Oh, but, Lily would say, there was her father; her home; even, had she dared to say it, her painting. But all this seemed so little, so virginal, against the other."

Lily's thoughts circle around her art and with equal irresolution around Mrs. Ramsay. Lily tries to dismiss her, tries to devalue "her limited old-fashioned ideas, her mania for marriage."

Lily tries through her art to subdue the power of Mrs. Ramsay but discovers that to subdue this power is impossible, even after Mrs. Ramsay is dead:

> To want and not to have—to want and want—how that wrung the heart, and wrung it again and again! Oh Mrs. Ramsay! she called out silently, to that essence which sat by the boat, that abstract one made of her, that woman in grey, as if to abuse her for having gone, and then having gone, to come back again. It had seemed so safe, thinking of her. Ghost, air, nothingness, a thing you could play with easily and safely at any time of day or night, she had been that, and then suddenly she put her hand out and wrung the heart thus. (266)

She tries to turn away from thoughts of Mrs. Ramsay to her painting, but finds that her vision is blurred by tears.

And here one must make sense of the shocking abruptness of Mrs. Ramsay's disappearance from the narrative. Ten years after the death of Mrs. Ramsay, the surviving characters reassemble at the house that has stood empty all this time. At the behest of Mr. Ramsay, James and Cam, the youngest son and daughter, undertake to complete with him the trip to the lighthouse that had been under discussion in the opening section. Here, finally, is the portrait of her father that Woolf had intended, as she began writing, to be the center of her book. Mr. Ramsay is indeed colossal in his self-absorption, insatiable in his needs, bearing down coercively on his children and on any woman from whom he might extort sympathy, surrounding his sorrow with "heavy draperies of grief" (227): Woolf uses the same image in the novel and in her memoir.

James and Cam, introduced as children in the first part of the novel, are now ten years older. They have been altered by grief.

James, the six-year-old contentedly cutting out pictures in the opening scene of intimacy with his mother, has grown up sullen. Silently watching his sister waver, tempted to break their pact of opposition to their father, he expects her to give way "as he watched a look come upon her face, a look he remembered. They look down he thought, at their knitting or something. Then suddenly they look up. There was a flash of blue, he remembered, and then somebody sitting with him laughed, surrendered, and he was very angry" (251). James, now sixteen, is remembering a scene that the reader, too, remembers. James's memory is blurred and impressionistic—"somebody sitting with him," "their knitting or something"—as a memory from the age of six may well be, but James is absolutely clear as to his own response: he was very angry. The memory that the reader knows to be particular, singular, has become, in his inner life, plural: "she" has become "they" as his memory of the scene with his mother has become an emblem for the perfidy of all women.

The event that we witnessed—the interruption, by his father, of his intimacy with his mother—is fused, for James, with the event we did not witness, his mother's death. The language of James's meditation is equivocal, encompassing equally both abandonments: the momentary one, the loss of his mother's attention when his father came and stood over them, and the permanent abandonment of her death.

Waiting for a breeze to stir the boat, James expects his father to express his impatience, "as, once before he had brought his blade down among them on the terrace and she had gone stiff all over, and if there had been an axe handy, a knife, or anything with a sharp point he would have seized it and struck his father through the heart. She had gone stiff all over, and then, her arm slackening, so that he felt she listened to him no longer, she had risen somehow and gone away and left him there, impotent, ridiculous, sitting on the floor grasping a pair of scissors" (277–

78). The phrase that is repeated, "she had gone stiff all over," refers to his mother's emotional response when his father appeared on the terrace—but in language that equally remembers her death. In James's memory of what happened when he was six, again the circumstances are vague—she had risen "somehow"— but his own affective state is absolutely clear: he felt impotent, ridiculous. James's loss—fusing his mother's death the moment when his father broke in on his intimacy with his mother—is conveyed in the simple immediacy of a child's language: "she listened to him no longer."

In the end, when at last James is praised by his father, he cannot allow his pride and pleasure to show. He must appear indifferent, hiding and hoarding his pleasure, as one does who has lived in an economy of scarcity.

Cam, too, is altered, but differently. As a child Cam had been the wild and defiant one, dashing past: she was the little girl who would not hand the gentleman the flower, as her nursemaid directed. She had clenched her fist and stamped. In the years that have passed since her mother's death, Cam's wildness has become subdued. Leaving the garden to enter the library of her father, she takes up a book and opens it, asking a question, doing what most pleases him and the other old gentlemen there. She cannot help admiring her father—finding him attractive, thinking him brave and adventurous—in spite of herself and in spite of her silent compact with her brother. On his side, her father tries to seduce her out of her withdrawal into engagement with him, questioning her about the puppy at home, and who will take care of it, and what will she call it. Observed through the eyes of her brother, Cam's face is sad and sulky and yielding. Together, brother and sister appear "a melancholy couple" as they come lagging after their father, "with a pallor in their eyes" that makes Lily Briscoe feel that "they suffered something beyond their years in silence."

But Woolf does more here than simply describe grief as it has left its stamp on a young son and daughter. What she does is to *induce* grief in the reader, to inflict it upon the reader. Over the course of the long first section, comprising more than half the novel, we have been drawn into its world, our own thoughts circling, like those of the characters, around the center of the book, Mrs. Ramsay. And then we turn the page, and she is gone. Everyone is gone. We find ourselves in the odd, impersonal prose of the second section, "Time Passes." A world that was vividly peopled, shifting from the subjectivity of one character to that of another, is suddenly empty. The prose has become stilted and self-consciously literary: the stylistic change creates a shock and catapults the reader into a strange, remote world. The desolate house with the wind blowing through it is an image of abandonment, but beyond this the stylistic change creates in the reader an *experience* of abandonment. It is as if our very interest, our engagement, were of no account.

The abrupt change is disorienting; we have lost our bearings. Where has everyone gone? Woolf induces in the reader something very like grief: confusion, dismay, loss, puzzlement, abandonment. And a sense that what remains, now, is something simply to be gotten through. One turns the pages of the book in order to finish what one has begun, but with the death of Mrs. Ramsay the life has gone from the novel itself.

Not only is Mrs. Ramsay gone, but her death itself is withheld in the narrative. As readers, we are shut out from witnessing it or even hearing it described. The death of Mrs. Ramsay is noted in a single sentence in brackets, indeed, in a subordinate clause within that bracketed sentence: "[Mr. Ramsay, stumbling along a passage one dark morning, stretched his arms out, but Mrs. Ramsay having died rather suddenly the night before, his arms, though stretched out, remained empty]" (194). This is all we are ever to learn about the death of Mrs. Ramsay.

It is a disturbing violation of our expectations. As readers we have been drawn into the fictional world of the novel and been led to feel entitled to more, to some explanation. Suddenly, it is as if our very interest were of no account or were dismissed with no acknowledgment. The withholding in the narrative of Mrs. Ramsay's death plays cruelly with the reader's emotional engagement by ignoring it completely. We are excluded, shut out, left to stumble about bewildered in the odd, stilted prose in which the passage of ten years is recorded.

Woolf does more here than simply describe varieties of grief, represented in the responses of the fictional characters to the death of the mother who is at the center of this work. Having begun the novel with a scene of intimacy between mother and child, having drawn the reader in not only to the child's point of view but with far greater immediacy to the child's mode of experience, the author turns the reader out into the cold, so to speak. She empties the landscape of people abruptly and without warning, in a way that is so indifferent, or so cruel, that it does not acknowledge the emotional engagement that is being betrayed. It is a hard look into the heart of a child's grief.

Her mother had died more than thirty years before Virginia Woolf wrote *To the Lighthouse*. Yet she felt that their relationship was altered by the writing of it: "I ceased to be obsessed by my mother. I no longer hear her voice; I do not see her." Until then, she says, she had felt haunted by her: "obsessed" is the word she uses, twice. "She obsessed me, in spite of the fact that she died when I was thirteen, until I was forty-four." Writing the novel affected her relationship with her father, too, more than two decades after his death: "Until I wrote it out, I would find my lips moving; I would be arguing with him; raging against him; saying to myself all that I never said to him . . . things it was impossible to say aloud" ("A Sketch of the Past," 108).

There is a crucial difference between the two accounts. In relation to her father, there were things it had been impossible to say aloud—but she was able to speak to him in her imagination, arguing and raging. With her mother, even in imagination Woolf condemned herself to silence. As she went about the activities of the day she could hear her mother's voice, see her, imagine what she would do or say. But it was only her mother who spoke. Woolf herself, whose letters and diaries fill many volumes, and these in addition to all of her fiction, essays, and reviews, was singularly mute.

Here I turn to another of Woolf's writings, the essay "Professions for Women." By the time she began to write, she says, it was a reputable occupation for a woman. But she found, nonetheless, that there was an obstacle:

> If I were going to review books I would need to do battle with a certain phantom. And the phantom was a woman, and when I came to know her better I called her after the heroine of a famous poem, The Angel in the House. . . . She was utterly unselfish. She excelled in the difficult arts of family life . . . she never had a mind or a wish of her own, but preferred to sympathize always with the minds and wishes of others. . . . I now record the one act for which I take some credit to myself. . . . I turned upon her and caught her by the throat. I did my best to kill her. . . . Had I not killed her she would have killed me. . . . whenever I felt the shadow of her wing or the radiance of her halo upon my page, I took up the inkpot and flung it at her. She died hard. Her fictitious nature was of great assistance to her. It is far harder to kill a phantom than reality. She was always creeping back when I thought I had despatched her.

Though I flatter myself that I killed her in the end, the struggle was severe. (*The Death of the Moth and Other Essays*, 236–38)

Woolf's language tries to be fanciful, but the figure is labored: she is killing someone who is already dead, variously described as angel, phantom, ghost. I am suggesting that killing the angel is what Woolf did in writing *To the Lighthouse*. And that this was how she silenced her mother at last.

Within the novel the death of the mother, which is omitted from the narrative, is in fact its central event. This fictional death was momentous for the author herself. In killing the angel in the house, Woolf finally broke her own silence in relation to her mother and gave voice to her rage, rage that she both inscribed and enacted in the novel.

But for all the violence of this passage, it still leaves things unsaid about Mrs. Ramsay and the book whose elusive center she is. In its fury and in its strong undertow of yearning, the novel raises questions past Virginia Woolf's own understanding. Like Lily Briscoe turning back to her canvas, Woolf's vision, I think, is blurred by tears.

Virginia Woolf asserted that in writing her autobiographical novel, she had "done for herself what psychoanalysts do for their patients." We read her statement written toward the end of her life, and of course we must demur. She was able to find some relief, evidently, in "silencing" the internal presence of her mother. What Woolf could not envisage, far less achieve, was a continuing relationship with the "invisible presence" of her mother, one in which her own voice could be heard as well as her mother's in ongoing counterpoint — a relationship of depth and complexity that would evolve throughout her life, as girl and woman.

2

The "Hyde Park Gate News"

Looking back to her childhood, whether in fiction or memoirs, Virginia Woolf was of course drawing on memories—and memories, she knew well, were subject to revision. She was acutely aware of the allusiveness and elusiveness of memory. But although Woolf herself could not look back on her early life except through the changing lens of memory, a remarkable document survives that allows us to recapture what she could not. Beginning in 1891, when Virginia was nine years old, she collaborated with Vanessa, Thoby, and Adrian on a family newspaper they called the "Hyde Park Gate News." What survives in its pages is the spirit of the Stephen family before the deaths that would follow, before the darkening and the silencing. The children's newspaper preserves the vitality of family life as it was lived in the present, rather than as seen through the mournful lens of retrospect. One discovers here the ordinary rhythms of family life humorously observed: the visits of relatives; April Fool's pranks; the loss of Thoby's boat in the Round Pond and its later return by the park keeper; the delight of Virginia and Vanessa when their piano teacher cancels a lesson; a stray dog adopted by the children; visits to the zoo; a picnic at Land's End.

Every Monday the newspaper appeared, its title penned in a large and grand script, at Christmastime in red ink, with "Christmas Number" emblazoned across the top. Carefully lettered, the various handwritings affirm that it was the product of a collaboration among the four children, though over time the handwriting, and the voice, become more recognizably those of Virginia. Week by week the children's newspaper chronicles the life of the Stephen family. Mixed in with family news are such special features as the occasional essay ("An Article on Chekiness"), a serialized story carried over from one issue to the next, and a delightfully imagined sequence of "Love Letters."[1]

It is not just intelligence and wit that are displayed here — though these shine through brilliantly at times — but exuberance and simple childish silliness: "Mr. C.D. Fischer has finished his stay of two days at 22 Hyde Park Gate. While he was there he amused the inhabitants much by making amusing grunts." The children who could be entertained by a cousin's grunts were also delighted by an April Fool's prank they played on their mother, delivering to her "a false epistle addressed to her on which was printed 'WE FOOLY WE FOOLY WE FOOLY BRED BUSSARD' by which familiar name she is generally known . . . Ha ha ha he he he laughed she with all the good-natured vehemence of her nature." What one discovers, in reading the "Hyde Park Gate News," is that laughter sounded through the rooms of 22 Hyde Park Gate, rooms that in Woolf's later accounts are darkened and silent.

A regular feature of the "Hyde Park Gate News" in its early numbers was a series of love letters. "These Love Letters," the authors explain, "are to show young people the right way to express what is in their hearts." One delightful exchange is that between Nora Howard and Tom Comton. Tom writes to his beloved, "My own sweet love Will you O will you wade down the stream of life with your would-be fiance who is waiting impa-

---

1. I have preserved, in this chapter, all childish misspellings to try to convey the pleasure of reading the "Hyde Park Gate News" as the children wrote it. Throughout the book I have also preserved, in quotations from Woolf's diaries and letters, her own spelling and idiosyncratic punctuation, again without editorial comment, which would interrupt the sound of her voice.

tiently out-side your hearts door he is waiting ever watching your least smile in his favour that may indicate pleasure at his being there." And Nora replies, "My own Tom, I love you with that fervent passion with which my father regards Roast beef but I do not look upon you with the same eyes as my father for he likes Roast Beef for its taste but I like you for your personal merits." In another issue, Roger Protheroe tries to woo the woman he loves by telling her that his father "has promised to give me £ 5000 to start me with and I have numerous aunts to die at any moment for my benefit." But Annie Foolhard declines, informing him that she is "engaged to another young fellow with twice your attracting and half your money."

The comings and goings of family members were always newsworthy events, embroidered with astute and amusing commentary about the character of these relatives. The paper carried a report of a visit by their cousin Millicent Vaughan: "Miss Vaughan has like a dutiful sister been to Canada to see her long absent sister who is residing there. We hope that no pangs of jealousy crossed her mind when she saw her sister so comfortably settled with a husband when she herself is searching the wide world in quest of matrimony." The children's own sibling rivalries are humorously reflected as well. When their grandmother comes to stay with them, the newspaper reports in Virginia's hand that "Mrs. Jackson has as no doubt our readers know brought her canary with her to Hyde Park Gate. It far excels in singing Miss Vanessa Stephen's bird." The youthful reporters take delight in tweaking their grandmother's proprieties: "There is a vulgar little song coming into fashion who's chorus is 'Ta ra ra bomteay.' We are sure that the proper mind of Mrs. Jackson would be properly shocked to know that this vulgar little ditty has actually been sung under the same house as the one in which she is."

One of the pleasures of reading the "Hyde Park Gate News"

is the discovery that the Stephen children were actually childish. They could laugh at their cousin's grunts and at a young lady's being seasick over the side of a boat. At St. Ives a friend of the family invited a group of young people to go fishing, and one of the party, a Miss Street, had never been out on the ocean before: "Many guesses were currant as to how she would undergo the trials awaiting her. She looked pale and showed all the usual signs of seasickness. . . . The giggling juveniles looked on at the first part of the scene but turned away from the second as Miss Street disgorged her contents much too liberally for the spectators."

It is a child's-eye view. The things that matter to children are what matter in the "Hyde Park Gate News"—an excursion to the zoo, the recovery of a lost toy sailboat. And food. Virginia, who in later periods of illness would sometimes refuse to eat, as a child had the reputation in her family for being especially enthusiastic about eating. To celebrate the birthdays of Stella and Vanessa, both of which fell in May, Mrs. Stephen and her three daughters visited Thoby's school to watch a cricket match. (His school won.) After the match, "they partook of a very slight refreshment though Mrs. Worsley on passing by remarked that Miss Virginia had taken in a good supply. But apparently Miss Virginia did not think so for she took another piece of cake as soon as she got home which she very soon did." When Vanessa and Virginia, "the two effeminate juveniles of 22 Hyde Park Gate" in the high-flown language of the "Hyde Park Gate News," went to the thirteenth birthday party of their neighbor, Miss Sybil Dilke, the newspaper carried this report: "When they arrived they found numerous other young ladies assembled. Soon after this tea was announced to the great joy of Miss Virginia Stephen. After tea which was very good they repaired to the drawing room to hear a ventriloquist who was amusing." And visiting their young neighbor again in June, the girls "went out into Kensington Gardens before tea and played many games. They went home and greatly to Miss Virginia's delight there were cherries for tea the first she had tasted this season." It is clear that Miss Virginia savored her cakes and her teas and her cherries.

Part of the humor of the "Hyde Park Gate News" comes from the attempt of the children to sound grown-up. They strain toward a larger vocabulary than they can comfortably wield and refer to all family members formally, with the prefixes Mr., Mrs., and Miss. The charm of the newspaper comes at times from the contrast between the high tone the descriptions aspire to and the delightful childishness of what is being described.

The settings of their activities, including the London zoo, where "the esteemed owner of the venerable mansion 22 Hyde Park Gate" took his nephew to see two new "ourangoutangs," and Kensington Gardens, where the children played games, suggest that although the children loved St. Ives best, London too had its pleasures. Leslie Stephen took the children to sail their toy boats in the Round Pond, and Thoby's boat, the *Thistle*, was lost for a time beneath the ice covering the pond. It was found and returned to its owner by the park keeper, who, in the London of 1892, would recognize the boat, know which child it belonged to and where his family lived, and appear at 22 Hyde Park Gate with the boat in hand. The return of the boat was a newsworthy event: "Last Saturday on going downstairs to tea Miss Virginia Stephen was called to the back door where her friend the genial faced park keeper stood holding the 'Thistle.' He explained that when the pond was being dragged of its weeds the boat had been found." Not to be outdone, Virginia relates in the next number of the "Hyde Park Gate News" a similar story of loss and recovery of her own boat. Her account begins with a dramatic flourish and broad calligraphic strokes: "Oh astounding event!!! 'The Fairy' has been restored to *terra firma* to the joy of her youthful owneress. It happened thus. Miss Virginia Stephen accompanied by the paterfamilias and her brother and sister visited the little pond having the intention to sail their miniature crafts." When she saw that her boat was being drawn up with weeds into the punt where workmen were standing, "she quickly told the parkkeeper who called on the punt and 'The Fairy' was quickly restored to her rightful owner."

Interestingly, it was Leslie Stephen who took the children to the pond with their boats, Leslie Stephen who took his nephew to the zoo to see the "ourangoutangs." In the pages of the "Hyde Park Gate News" Julia Stephen is a more peripheral figure in the day-to-day lives of the children. There is only one occasion reported when Virginia spends time with her mother: they make a court appearance concerning a neighbor's dog. The article describing the event is unquestionably by Virginia because at the time of the court appearance the other members of the family had all gone to a comedy. The account is dated January 18, 1892, a week before Virginia's tenth birthday:

> The long adjourned trial of the "Big Dog" as all the Stephens call it has at last come off to the great delight of Miss Virginia Stephen who went with her Mother to the Police Court on Saturday to bear testimony that the dog had flown at her. When they arrived at the Police Court they found they were rather early but a policeman told them to come with him into another appartment where they enjoyed warmth and comfort for about a minute when Mrs. MacKensie came into the same room. They had hardly been seated half a minute when a policeman announced that they were wanted. Mr. Martin was called up first but nothing much was made out of him. Then Miss Virginia Stephen was called up and

she stated that the dog had run at her and bitten her cloak besides knocking her up against the wall. Mrs. Stephen was called up and said that the dog had run up against her and she asked the young women who reside in the house to call their dog in and they said "No." She again asked if they would be so kind as to call their dog in. They replied "No" again. Mrs. Stephen returned to the bench on which they had been sitting. Mr. MacKensie's maid next was called up and state that the dog had flown at her whereupon the magistrate desired to know what was meant by "flown." The maid got very red and remained silent. The case ended by the magistrate saying the dog must either be killed or kept under proper control.

This highly detailed report shows the author's pleasure in the very telling of the event, in narration itself, in the particulars that give vividness to any account. As early as age nine, Virginia was a writer and was recognized as such by her family. Their presents for her tenth birthday, reported in the next issue, make this clear: "She is the happy possessor of a beautiful inkstand the gift of her Grandmother. . . . She had also a blotter a drawing-book a box with writing impleements inside." Whether for her birthday or when George and Stella Duckworth return from a trip abroad, inkstands and writing implements are the gifts her family gives to Virginia.

In the rhythms of the children's life, the adoption of a stray dog is an event of some magnitude and is told lovingly and charmingly over several issues of the "Hyde Park Gate News." The first report appears in the issue of February 22, 1892: "The juveniles of 22 Hyde Park Gate on going home last Monday espied a small brown mongrel in the street. They naturally went up to him and passed their hands carressingly over his back." Not surprisingly, the stray followed the children home, "and he has resided with the Stephens until the present day." By the next issue, a week later, the dog has been given a name and has become part of the children's life in London. The newspaper carried their proud description: "The aforementioned dog called Beauty possesses a remarkable attraction for other members of the canine tribe. When she goes out for walks if one of the young Stephens carries her other dogs come round the person who is so doing casting many wistful looks and sniffs in the direction of Beauty."

However many wistful looks and sniffs Beauty received, Julia Stephen was not among her admirers. Indeed, her "one warmest desire was to get rid of the dog although she is an adorer of the canine tribe in general but her dislike is most centered in him for he is not renowned for cleanliness." (Apparently the dog changed its gender, in the eyes of the children, when it was messy.) Sadly for the children, another home had to be found for the stray, who "said good bye in it's mute way to the shelter of 22 Hyde Park Gate."

Saying goodbye to Beauty, "that glowing emblem of the canine tribe," was not, however, the end of the dog story. Later that year, when the family was settled for the summer in St. Ives, Mrs. Stephen was "riled" to find that rats were eating their provisions. The solution: to have a dog after all. Gerald, who was still in London, was commissioned to get an Irish terrier, and the "Hyde Park Gate News" for July 11, 1892, describes the arrival of this addition to the Stephen household:

> Great excitement has pervaded the household of Mr. Leslie Stephen on account of the beautiful Irish terrier which as we have mentioned in our last number Mrs. Stephen asked Mr. Gerald Duckworth to

procure as he is in London. The juveniles went down anxiously to meet every possible train by which the darling dog could arrive. They were disappointed by one train but the ideal beauty came by the second train. Mrs. Stephen and Miss Stella Duckworth came and waited on the steps which lead down to the terminus and Mr. Stephen actually came to the terminus itself as he could not withstand the anxiety and excitement which reigned omnipotent.

The dog's appellation is Shag a derivation from Shaggy as he is long-haired and numerous haired. He is grey. He is extremely affectionate especially toward Mrs. Stephen. The chief reason why he was obtained was that he might consume the rats of which we have spoken in a former number. He is very obedient and docile which united with a loveable temper will make him a favourite wherever he goes.

This account of the arrival of the "darling dog" forms itself into a tableau, a picture of life at St. Ives: the children meeting every possible London train, eagerly awaiting the arrival of the dog Gerald has chosen, Mrs. Stephen and Stella waiting on the steps to the train terminus, Mr. Stephen coming to the terminus itself, participating fully in the excitement of the children.

For the reader who knows the family as it was portrayed in Woolf's later accounts, the picture has some surprises. One is the tone of the relations between the Duckworths and the rest of the family at this time. The comings and goings of George and Gerald are reported in these pages as part of the natural rhythms of family life. Gerald stages a "splendid display of fireworks" at St. Ives every September to celebrate Thoby's birthday, to the "super-exuberance" of the children. On a walk with

Leslie Stephen, when the children find a bird tangled in a fishing net it is Gerald who "skilfully extricates" the bird, saving its life. For entertainment the family played tableaus: one evening George and Stella burst into laughter and "set the audience off laughing until the whole house rang again. The whole thing was pronounced a success." The contagiousness of laughter suggests an ease in one another's presence.[2]

To return to the scene at the St. Ives train station: the picture of Julia Stephen coming with the family but remaining apart resonates with Woolf's later accounts. Julia will no doubt greet Gerald lovingly when the train arrives; in the "Hyde Park Gate News" whenever Gerald returns she has tears of joy in her eyes. Indeed, the reader begins to see that Julia is rather more loving to her sons than to her daughters. When Gerald first returns at end of term from Cambridge, "his mother stood fondly gasing at him her beautiful eyes which were expressive of doubt whether he were the same substantial being who had left for Cambridge only a few months before." And three months later, "Mr. Gerald Duckworth came home on Wednesday to the great joy of all. Our author was much touched to see tears in the maternal eyes." On the occasion of George's twenty-fourth birthday, "he accompanied his Mother to see her beloved Thoby" at his school. The reporter comments, "It must indeed be sad for the Mother to see her sons growing older and older and then to watch them leave the sweet world of child-hood behind them and enter into the great world of manhood." In contrast, the "Hyde Park Gate News" does not record any signs of special affection, ever, toward her daughters Virginia or Vanessa or Stella.

2. Much has been written about Woolf's later allegations in relation to her half-brothers, so much that, as Lee (1996) points out, it has become impossible to consider the issue apart from all that has been made of it. See her thoughtful discussion of the complexities of the matter, 144–56.

Julia's coddling of her youngest son, Adrian, was apparently notorious in the family. In the issue of the "Hyde Park Gate News" for February 1, 1892, Mrs. Stephen is reported to have a lingering concern about Adrian's "little cold," though it is obvious to all other members of the family that he was never very sick to begin with and is now entirely better. And when Adrian caught cold again, his mother's tender administering of medicine is gently mocked by whichever of his siblings wrote this account: "It is indeed a pretty sight to see the Mother holding the spoon between her slim fingers and the uplifted and eager face of the little one whose pretty cherub lips are parted ready to recieve the tit-bits from the fond Mother." A pretty sight indeed. Twice Adrian tried to start a newspaper of his own to rival the "Hyde Park Gate News"—first it was the "Talland Gazette" and later the "Corkscrew Gazette"—but his efforts met little success. The editor of the "Hyde Park Gate News" (at this point, clearly it was Virginia) drew herself up to her full height and gave his endeavor her patronizing encouragement: "We hope that it will get the success it deserves. It will not be underrated by Mrs. Stephen nor overrated by Mr. Stephen." Pithily she conveys the mother's idealization of her son—and the father's skepticism about his talents.

That Julia Stephen favored her sons over her daughters is perhaps not surprising. What does come as a surprise is the way Leslie Stephen comes to life in the pages of the "Hyde Park Gate News." He is altogether different from the brooding, morose, self-pitying man Woolf later described—deaf to all but his own needs. Rather, this Leslie Stephen is a man of considerable vitality, very much engaged in the day-to-day life of his family. Waiting for the arrival of the new dog, he does not stay back on the steps with Julia and Stella but joins the children on the train platform, where "excitement reigned omnipotent." And he took pleasure in sharing his interests with his children, taking them for a walk to the peninsula to see the waves, finding a bird's nest and later bringing them back to revisit it. When he took the younger children to watch George and Gerald play golf, he pointed out to them along the way "the interesting sight of a raven pursuing a hawk. The hawk with one swoop flew ahead but the raven with a few steady strokes of his strong wings came up beside the other bird of prey and chased him away. This spectacle was enjoyed by both Father and children." As the sharply etched detail of the description suggests, Leslie Stephen taught his children to observe nature closely. He collected flowers with them and encouraged them to learn the names of plants. The children's own zestful pleasure in collecting butterflies and moths, an activity they all participated in for many years, saving their treasures in their "bug box," is a reflection of interests they first developed with their father. He is recognized by his children to be a man of accomplishment: when he receives an honorary degree from Cambridge, when he is named president of the London Library, the occasions are recorded with pride. As he appears in the "Hyde Park Gate News" Leslie Stephen is not the remote figure of Woolf's retrospective accounts. Later in her life, she would look back on this time and write that it seemed that not one but two generations separated the Stephen children from their parents. In the pages of the "Hyde Park Gate News," Leslie Stephen, joining his children on the train platform when they were unable to contain their excitement at the arrival of their new dog, seems as eager as the children themselves.

Two incidents recorded in these pages will sound familiar to readers of *To the Lighthouse*. Both take place at St. Ives. This was the place the children loved best, as is evident from an item in the "Hyde Park Gate News" of May 16, 1892:

> The first ices of the season were eaten on Wednesday by Miss Minna Duckworth. The Ices were esccep-

tionally exceptionable on that day as it was hot and sultry. That day is stamped deeply in the minds of the juveniles for two things. The first was the ices and the second was that Madame Mao who we may as well inform our readers is the Stephen's instructress in the art of music was to come twice a week!!! But this blow was very much softened by the fact that the Stephens were going to St. Ives very much earlier than usual. This is a heavenly prospect.

One of the pleasures of St. Ives was the annual regatta, held in mid-August. This year, however, there was some discussion of whether it might be raining too hard for the regatta to take place. The discussion, back and forth, anticipates the opening scene of *To the Lighthouse*, in which his mother tells James, "Yes, of course, if it's fine tomorrow," and his father spoils his happiness by saying definitively, "But . . . it won't be fine." In the Stephen family discussion, however, it was Mrs. Stephen who remonstrated that it was pouring and argued against their going, while Mr. Stephen, along with the children, was eager to go regardless of the weather. In spite of his wife's protestations he took the children to the regatta, and when in the course of the afternoon it began to rain again he decided, to the great joy of the children, that they would all stay on anyway.

Another excursion will also remind readers of a scene in *To the Lighthouse*. At the end of the summer at St. Ives, Stephen took his youngest son and daughter out in a boat. How different this excursion is from the mournful one that ends the novel. Stephen, Adrian, and Virginia "went down to the pier and there looked about for a boat. After a long time of waiting a man appeared. They were soon out and sailing merrily along. There was a good breeze and it not being too calm the party was in high spirits." The high-spirited party described in the pages of the children's newspaper would be transformed, in fiction, to the mournful, unwilling excursion of Mr. Ramsay and the sullen James and Cam, returning to the empty house after the death of their mother. Preserved in the pages of the "Hyde Park Gate News" is a picture of family life that is robust, exuberant, and merry—before it would be shattered by death and before memory itself would be colored by grief and rage.

3

Diary, Age Fifteen

"A VOLUME OF FAIRLY ACUTE LIFE"

In *To the Lighthouse,* Virginia Woolf ascribes to her fictional surrogate, the painter Lily Briscoe, the thought, "A brush, the one
dependable thing in a world of strife, ruin, chaos." If one substi-
tutes "pen" for "brush," these words might well be an epigraph
for the diary that Virginia Woolf kept when she was fifteen years
old. The diary is, as she wrote in drawing it to a close, "a volume
of fairly acute life." As a documentation of family life, the diary
could be said to resume the narrative begun in the pages of the
"Hyde Park Gate News." Clever, irreverent, high-spirited, the
children's newspaper records and preserves a vibrant family life
in weekly issues over 1891 and 1892. And then there is a marked
change of tone. The issues for 1893 and 1894 have unfortunately
been lost; the extant sequence resumes with the issue of January 7, 1895. Over the following months the newspaper reports a
winter of severe cold, frozen pipes, illness. A measles epidemic at
Adrian's school forced him to come home early, and Thoby had
to return from Cambridge because of an epidemic of influenza.
Then Julia Stephen became ill. Several issues of the "Hyde Park
Gate News" carry optimistic reports of her improvement, until
the last issue, that of Monday, April 8, 1895. The "Hyde Park
Gate News" stopped abruptly as her illness became more grave.
On May 5, 1895, Julia died. Soon afterward, Virginia had her
first breakdown. She was thought still to be convalescing from
this breakdown when on January 3, 1897, she began keeping the
diary I want to consider here.

Years later, Woolf looked back on the beginning of the family's emergence from the terrible darkness that followed the death of her mother. In writing of it, she distilled that complex process into a particular moment. One day before going back to school, Thoby had said, "'It's silly going on like this . . .', sobbing, sitting shrouded, he meant. I was shocked at his heartlessness; yet he was right, I know; and yet how could we escape? It was Stella who lifted the canopy again. A little light crept in" ("A Sketch of the Past," 95). Stella, Virginia's half-sister, the daughter of her mother's first marriage, was twenty-five years old when Julia Stephen died. It was Stella who stepped into the place of woman of the house after the death of their mother, running the household, looking after the children, attending to the abundant needs of Leslie Stephen. This is the time in the life of the family when the diary of Virginia begins.

For the reader who opens this volume with curiosity about her inner life, the diary is at first glance a disappointment. It is a *journal*, begun with the new year, and for the most part it is a record of events. A diary that is a record of one's inner life will have some entries that are longer than others: there are days when the mind teems with thoughts and observations and other days that are arid. What one first notices on opening this diary is that there is an entry for every day and that the entries are of uniform length. There is not the expansiveness one would see, just by the appearance of the diary, on a day when a new thought takes hold of the imagination and one page flows onto the next. There is not the hiatus of a day or a few days when the events of life become so exciting that the recording of them must wait. Rather, this is a more rigid enterprise—or tries to be.

The entry dated Friday, January 22, 1897, three days before Virginia's fifteenth birthday, suggests the pattern of life at this time:

Nessa went to her drawing. Stewart arrived here at 11, and he and Thoby went to see Lord Leightons pictures. Stella and I went to Soars with a photograph, to Aldous'es for some flowers for Lisas tea party, and to the Gloucester Rd. Station about As season ticket, which is now finally disposed of. Outside the station we met Mr Gibbs, and Stella taking the green bus to go to Cousin Mias, he walked all the way back home with me. It began to snow, and he made me hold his arm, and trot along under his umbrella. He promised to come round on Monday morning—Aunt Mary sent me, as a birthday present, a case of jams—10 pots of jam—four of which I have kept, the rest, being nasty ones, were given to Thoby. It snowed all the afternoon, and Nessa and I did not go out—Thoby and Stewart went to the Animatograph at the Polytechnic, and came back here at 4. Tea for them was at 4.15, and at a quarter to 5, they started for Clifton. Nessa and I had a quiet tea alone, though not allowed to read—After tea, Nessa drew at the "Oak Davenport" which holds all our paper now and is very nice, and I wrote on a table beside her. Florence Maitland came to tea, sobbing for her monkey, which Fred had made her sell—She wished to rebuy it on the way home, but Gerald, who went to the station with her, forbade this—Harry Stephen for dinner. Jack had to go out on business. (*A Passionate Apprentice*, 19)

Typically on weekdays Virginia's half-brothers, George and Gerald, would leave for work after breakfast, and her younger brother Adrian would set off for Westminster School. Thoby was at Clifton College in Bristol. On Mondays, Wednesdays, and Fridays, her sister Vanessa would bicycle to her art classes. Her father usually went for a walk with Virginia in the morning, weather permitting, then retired to his study to work. This left Virginia at home with Stella, and she spent most of these days trotting along with Stella on the errands of a busy household.

"Not allowed to read," Virginia mentions in passing. A week later she records a visit to Dr. Seton which clarifies this puzzling statement. Her lessons had been stopped—and bicycling forbidden—since the summer of 1895 and the breakdown that followed her mother's death. Exercise, it was thought, would do her good, exercise in the wholesome outdoors, and thus the walk each morning with her father and again several hours out of doors every afternoon, most often accompanying Stella.

In the context of this regimen, the very factuality of her journal begins to be more interesting. This diary reflects precisely an effort *not* to be swept away by her inner life, but rather to hold on, as firmly as she can, to external reality. The uniform length of the entries, day by day, is a requirement she insisted upon for herself: a brittle rigidity that is hinted at just by the look of the page and confirmed by the occasional entry in which she writes explicitly of not knowing how to fill up the remaining space, or not having had room, the previous day, for something she had wanted to set down. The very factuality of the journal reflects her effort to hold onto the world of ordinary experience and, more particularly, to fix it in place by its representation in words; it had proved too fluid already and would threaten to become so again, over the course of this year.

Woolf spoke explicitly of this matter in her diary many years later, again at a time when her hold on ordinary reality was faltering. In the entry for March 8, 1941, in what would prove to be her penultimate diary entry, she wrote, "Haddock and sausage meat. I think it is true that one gains a certain hold on sausage and haddock by writing them down" (*Diary* 5:358). This is precisely what the fifteen-year-old Virginia tries to do here—to "gain a certain hold" on the external world, on the quotidian facts of life, by writing them down.

Even so, there are enthusiasms and pleasures. Her birthday fell several weeks after she began keeping the diary: "Father finished Esmond to us this evening—His present for me came—Lockhart's Life of Scott—in a great brown paper parcel—I expected one huge closely printed book, but instead behold 10 beautiful little blue and brown gilt leathered backs, big print, and altogether luxurious. The nicest present I have had yet" (22). Note the pleasure, the physicality, the sensuousness of this description and compare it with the listing of her other presents the previous day: "Stella and I went to Story's to buy me an arm chair, which is to be Ss present to me—We got a very nice one, and I came straight home, while Stella went on to Wimpole St. Gerald gave me £1, and Adrian a holder for my stylograph . . . Cousin Mia gave me a diary and another pocket book. Thoby writes to say that he has ordered films for me" (21–22). She is pleased by these presents, but no gift other than her father's is lingered over, savored.

Her sensual appreciation of her father's gift glows through diary entries over the following days: "Went up to read with father, and then began my beloved Lockhart—which grows more and more beautiful every day." And in a letter to Thoby: "Gradually all my presents have arrived—Fathers Lockhart came the evening I wrote to you—ten most exquisite little volumes, half bound in purple leather, with gilt scrolls and twirls and thistles everywhere, and a most artistic blue and brown mottling on their other parts. So my blinded eyesight is poring more fervidly than ever over miserable books—only not even you, my dear brother, could give such an epithet to these lovely creatures"

(*Letters* 1:4). Exquisite little volumes, lovely creatures that grow more and more beautiful every day: these are indeed treasured gifts to a daughter from her father.

Books were their special bond. At fifteen Virginia Woolf was an astonishing reader. Having begun her diary at the new year, she records that on January 5 she has just finished volume 1 of *Three Generations of English Women* and has begun volume 2. By January 7 she has finished the second volume and has begun Froude's *Life of Carlyle*. On January 9 she has finished the first volume of this biography, and by January 14 the second. She began Thackeray's *The Newcomes* on January 23, and on her birthday, January 25, she was "Reading four books at once—The Newcomes, Carlyle, Old Curiosity Shop, and Queen Elizabeth—" (22). By January 27 she has finished the first volume of Carlyle's *Reminiscences;* by the thirtieth, she has finished the second volume. And on the thirty-first she begins reading her "beloved Lockhart," the ten-volume biography of Sir Walter Scott that was her father's birthday gift.

"Gracious, child, how you gobble," Leslie Stephen would say to her. And in his memoir, begun after the death of Julia, "Ginia is devouring books, almost faster than I like." It is, it seems, the inevitable metaphor. In her own memoir, Woolf describes herself reading Boswell as "gnawing my way through the eighteenth century" ("A Sketch of the Past," 157). And as a girl she uses a similar figure here, but idiosyncratically. On June 3, she notes that she is reading Carlyle's Cromwell and describes it as "harder to get on with than the French Revolution but better than some other works that I have had to devour" (95).

"Have had to devour," she says—a curious construction. The phrase seems self-contradictory. The verb "to devour" has the urgency of being impelled from within, by extreme hunger; but "have had to" suggests acquiescence or reluctant submission. We have all, at times, had to swallow things we did not want to, but devouring is not ordinarily something forced. The odd construction suggests how driven her behavior was, how impelled it was by inner necessity.

"Gracious, child, how you gobble." Stephen's words show unmistakable approval and affection for the daughter whose love of books reflected his own. Books were the gifts her father gave her, they were her bond with him, they were her sustenance, feverishly devoured. And books gave her refuge: "My dear Pepys is the only calm thing in the house" (66).

Virginia wrote this at a time when the household was topsy-turvy, bustling with preparations. The following Saturday was to be Stella's wedding day, and the last weeks had been taken up with the sending of invitations, the trying on of dresses, the buying of presents, the arrival of flowers, everything leading up to the date when Stella and Jack Hills would be married.

Jack Hills had for some years been Stella's patient, persistent suitor. She had refused him in the past; with her mother's death and her taking on the responsibilities of a busy household, marriage had seemed all the more out of the question. Certainly it was so to Leslie Stephen, who needed Stella. Jack Hills persisted, however, and one evening the previous August he and Stella had returned from a walk and announced that they were engaged. In Woolf's later recollection of this period, she emphasizes her father's unreasonable resistance to Stella's proposed marriage. What her fifteen-year-old diary reveals, however, is her own sense of imminent loss. In its pages readers may trace her response to that loss, but only by reading between the lines.

Stella and Jack's wedding day was to be April 10, 1897. By late March it seemed that the world was increasingly filled with danger. On March 24, Virginia records in her diary "the most fiendish March wind that ever blew." Two days later, she writes that she saw a lady bicyclist run over by a cart. On March 31, when Vanessa bicycled to the studio as she did every Monday, Wednesday, and Friday, Virginia found it worth recording in her diary that her sister had met with no accident.

Now the streets of London became "perilous crossings" from which Virginia is "thankful to get home safe at all." She alludes to her own anger just once ("To bed very furious and tantrumical"); more characteristically it is projected upon the external world, transforming it into a scene of malevolence. The streets are "in the most fiendish state of uproar"; the weather is "behaving in the most diabolical manner"; there is a "violent shower of drizzle"; the wind is "diabolical as usual"; it is "as ferocious as ever." The only refuge in this storm is that which she finds in books: "Several times I was blown into hedges, & the bicycles behaved in a most drunk way—lurching from side to side—Home safely after a rather horrible expedition—Began 2nd vol. of Macaulay." There is an almost audible sigh of relief as she opens her Macaulay.

In the weeks of preparation for Stella's wedding, Virginia allows herself to alight only momentarily on her fears, the allusion almost buried in the account of busy activity: "In the morning we went to Mrs. Roberts in Westbourne Grove—Margaret was not there this time. We had our linings tried on—I was forced to wear certain underclothing for the first time in my life—All the invitations were finished and sent off in the morning—so that theres an end of that job—Only ten days now to the wedding—what will become of us—In the afternoon we shopped in High St" (64). The entry continues with a record of the afternoon's shopping, who came to tea, and who came to dinner. It ends, again with palpable relief, "Began Caesar."

The wedding preparations continued, the "hurly burly" went on to the last minute of finishing touches by florists and hairdressers. And then the day itself: "There was a long service—then it was all over—Stella and Jack were married—We went up and saw her change her dress—and said goobye to her. So they went—Mr. and Mrs. Hills!"

Stella and Jack went to Italy on their honeymoon, and Leslie Stephen, with Vanessa, Thoby, Virginia, and Adrian, went on holiday to Brighton. They returned to London on April 28 and were met at Victoria Station by George, who told them that Stella had come back from her honeymoon ill. The next day she was diagnosed with peritonitis.

From the first Virginia was alarmed, as she read the signs. Dr. Seton came three times the first day, a nurse was hired, and then another, and straw was laid down on the road, as was customarily done to deaden the noise of carts and carriages outside houses in which there was serious illness: "No getting rid of the thought—all these ghastly preparations add to it—the people jar at every possible occasion. I slept with Nessa, as I was unhappy. News that she is better at about 11 o'clock. What shall I write tomorrow?" Stella seemed at first to be getting better. Three days after their return to London Virginia wrote in her diary, "For the first time since Wednesday, I read quietly and happily at my cherished Macaulay. After all books are the greatest help and comfort." For the first two nights, feeling sad and frightened, she had slept with Vanessa. Then she returned to sleeping alone and began, each night, to take a book to bed with her.

From the time the diagnosis of peritonitis was made on April 29, the diary, which keeps its gaze directed outward, again records a world full of danger, mirroring her own vivid sense of the precariousness of life and her rage projected onto the streets of London. She notes, amid the comings and goings of the household, "a week of ferocious carriage wheels and accidents": "We saw a hansom overturned in Piccadilly—I saw it in mid air— the horse lifted from its legs, and the driver jumping from the box. Luckily neither horse nor driver suffered though the hansom was broken—Then again, I managed to discover a man in the course of being squashed by an omnibus, but, as we were in the midst of Piccadilly Circus, the details of the accident could not be seen" (82–83). And again, while waiting in a confectioners for some sponge cakes for Stella's tea,

> I heard a stampede in the street outside—shouting —as the stampede became more violent—& then a crash. Evidently the runaway had collided. A glimpse out of the door—to which the young ladies all crowded to get a better view—showed one horse on the ground and a second prancing madly above it —a carriage was smashed up & a wagon turned over on to its side. The young ladies were dispersed by the appearance of an infuriated steed at the door— pushing it with its nose; however he was captured in time. As soon as things were quieter we fled— without the sponge cakes—No one hurt. (85)

The infuriated steed, the violent stampede, the ferocious carriage wheels, the horse prancing madly: a world charged with rage is a dangerous place in which to make one's way.

Occasionally Virginia uses the diary to record directly her mood: "We went round in the morning & saw Stella. I was extremely gruff & unpleasant, which, however, is to be ascribed to the effect of the hot weather on my nerves—Nothing else!" Her conjunction "however" and her emphatic "Nothing else!" of course imply alternative explanations, which she pointedly deflects. She is full of helpless rage: Stella is dying, and Virginia seems to know this or to fear it from the outset.

But then Stella seemed to rally and was allowed to go out for the first time. After several days of encouraging reports, Virginia wrote in her journal, "Nessa went in to see Stella this morning. She was struck by her looks: fatter decidedly than after the wedding & looking altogether better—This is most satisfactory—but I am unreasonable enough to be irritated" (80). The signs of improvement, too, may have angered Virginia by their bitter contrast with her mother's course. In her diary she quickly changes the subject from her own "unreasonable" irritation to record the round of afternoon errands. The date of this entry, May 4, is one day before the date of her mother's death two years earlier, an anniversary to which she would remain attuned throughout her life. Her entry for the date itself, May 5, begins with a long description of a fire at a charity bazaar in Paris, at which two hundred people were killed, and she writes of the "ghastly details" in the newspapers. The victims claimed by the fire were charitable ladies engaged in doing good, ladies not unlike her mother.

There is indeed in this diary an occasional glimpse of undisguised venomousness, even sadism. Invariably it is directed against an older woman. There is a "horrid skinny little lady, an old hag" from whom she and Stella get a reference for a prospective cook at Stella's new home. There is a "wheezy old lady" in the row in front of them when the Stephen children attend the reading of the banns for Stella and Jack, who follows the choristers "in a toothless tuneless whistle." Returning from a walk on the day before the anniversary of her mother's death, Virginia sees a "hideous set of bedecked old frumps." Three days later, a "Mrs. Green—that wicked old harpy—as for the future I shall call her—came to see Father." In the diaries and letters of her adult years, this aspect of Woolf's character is modulated to a sort of zestful maliciousness that makes these volumes delicious reading; here, there is no pleasure either for the writer or for the reader.

Over the period of apprehension and watchfulness, the diary registers her awareness that the perceptual world was becoming more difficult to hold onto. Virginia tries to maintain the factuality that has characterized this diary from the beginning, but now she is not always able to: "Nessa went to the drawing. Father & I began our morning pond walks. Afterward I sat with Stella, & then went out to High St, & bought some grapes (I think—today is rather vague, as I most disgracefully forgot to write for two days). After luncheon—(This is all mixed up with Thursday—) I cannot remember at all what happened in the afternoon; but I think I shopped in High St—A most dreadful failure—" (83-84). And again, "I went out to Herbert & Jones for Stella, & bought sponge cakes. Nessa at her drawing. I cannot remember what happened to me in the afternoon—I think I went out somewhere but I forget any thing about it" (99-100).

The precariousness of Virginia's state was apparently becoming evident to others. Her diary records that on May 9 Dr. Seton ordered that she have milk, medicine, and exercise out of doors —and that her lessons, which had been resumed in February, be stopped. Again and again over the course of her lifetime, she would be deprived on therapeutic grounds of precisely that which was most soothing, most reliable, most comforting to her.

Over the following weeks Stella's condition grew worse. On July 19, at three o'clock in the morning, George and Vanessa came to Virginia's room to tell her that Stella had died. Three months after her wedding, Stella was buried beside her mother.

The death of Stella, terrible in itself, must also have been a nightmare reprise for Virginia of her mother's death two years earlier. The family physician who attended Stella was the same physician who had attended Julia Stephen through her final illness. Indeed, he is the central figure in Woolf's memory of the death of her mother. This passage is from a diary entry written when she was forty-two years old:

> May 5, 1924. This is the 29th anniversary of mothers death. I think it happened early on a Sunday morn-

ing, & I looked out of the nursery window & saw old Dr Seton walking away with his hands behind his back, as if to say It is finished, & then the doves descending, to peck in the road, I suppose, with a fall & descent of infinite peace. I was 13, & could fill a whole page & more with my impressions of that day, many of them ill received by me, & hidden from the grown ups, but very memorable on that account: how I laughed, for instance, behind the hand which was meant to hide my tears; & through the fingers saw the nurses sobbing (*Diary* 2:300).

It is a visual memory that has the force of metaphor, distilling into a single image disparate and even contradictory currents of feeling. Her remembered laughter, hidden behind her hand, is a defiant note, her protest against the hypocrisies and conventions of sorrow—having been "made to act parts that we did not feel; to fumble for words that we did not know." Perhaps, too, her remembered laughter registers her ambivalence toward the mother she lost so early, and had never really had.

Woolf would write again in her diary, ten years later, her memories of her mother's death. Now she remembers herself secretly laughing *at* the nurse who was crying: "She's pretending, I said: aged 13." This was written just after the death of her friend Roger Fry, in 1934: she was reminded of her mother's death and was afraid, now as then, that she was not feeling enough. In the same diary entry, however, she goes on to describe unmistakable symptoms of depression: "I feel dazed: very wooden. . . . And I'm too stupid to write anything. My head all stiff. I think the poverty of life now is what comes to me. a thin blackish veil over everything. . . . The substance gone out of everything (*Diary* 4:242).

In her memoir, in a passage dated May 2, 1939, she returns to the scene she had described in her diary on the anniversary of her mother's death, fifteen years earlier. Again she remembers herself leaning out the nursery window and seeing Dr. Seton walking away. Now she adds another image: "George took us down to say goodbye. My father staggered from the bedroom as we came. I stretched out my arms to stop him but he brushed past me, crying out something I could not catch; distraught. And George led me in to kiss my mother, who had just died" (91). The poignant gesture of the daughter, which went unnoticed by her grief-struck father, would become that of Mr. Ramsay after the death of his wife, stumbling along a passage: his arms "though stretched out, remained empty."

"How that early morning picture has stayed with me!" she observes. In the scene in her mind's eye, the receding solitary figure of Dr. Seton, his head bent and hands clasped behind his back, would seem to personify for a child of thirteen the terrible helplessness of adults in the face of illness and death. The diary entry of May 5, 1924, was written twenty-nine years after the event, and the remembered figure of Dr. Seton had accrued additional layers of meaning in retrospect. Between the death of her mother and the writing of these memories, there were other illnesses, other deaths. Dr. Seton remained the family physician through the death of Stella and that of Leslie Stephen; it was he who ordered that Virginia's lessons be stopped during the breakdown after her mother's death and again when Stella was ill. Over the course of Virginia's lifetime there would be other Dr. Setons, equally impotent. In her experience they were helpless to prevent the deaths of those she loved and needed and helpless, too, in the face of her own recurrent episodes of depression and psychosis.

In the memoir that Virginia Woolf left unfinished at her death, she looked back on the impact of her mother's death when she was thirteen and that of Stella when she was fifteen:

My mother's death had been a latent sorrow—at thirteen one could not master it, envisage it, deal with it. But Stella's death two years later fell on a different substance; a mind stuff and being stuff that was extraordinarily unprotected, unformed, unshielded. . . . That must always hold good of minds and bodies at fifteen. But beneath the surface of this particular mind and body lay sunk the other death. Even if I were not fully conscious of what my mother's death meant, I had been for two years unconsciously absorbing it through Stella's silent grief; through my father's demonstrative grief; again through all the things that changed and stopped . . . when once more unbelievably—incredibly—as if one had been violently cheated of some promise; more than that, brutally told not to be such a fool as to hope for things; I remember saying to myself after she died: "But this is impossible; things aren't, can't be, like this"—the blow, the second blow of death, struck on me; tremulous, filmy eyed as I was, with my wings still creased, sitting there on the edge of my broken chrysalis. ("A Sketch of the Past," 124)

It is a passage of astonishing power. Knowing that within months of writing this she would commit suicide by drowning herself, we register the prescience of her metaphor, with its unwitting revelation: her mother's death, she wrote, "lay sunk" beneath the surface.

Stella's was "the second blow of death," Woolf says, and she was still reeling from the first when she began to keep her journal. Given the dark period in which the journal was begun and the terrible events that would unfold, it is remarkable to discover that there is always a tone of pleasure surrounding the *act of writing* itself. The very implements of writing are endowed with spirit, with animation. The texture of the paper, the particular pen, the width of the nib, even the blotting pad, all are lingered over in the description, and savored: "My old board has been restocked with blotting paper, and made to look youthful once more, and I use it with great joy after tea, so that Mr Gibbs (blotter) has been removed to the day nursery for scrappiness—whence it comes to pass that I am using him now." This enthusiasm, even playfulness, would be sustained through the darkening weeks and months that followed, but specifically and solely in relation to writing.

"Using *him*," she writes of her blotter. She often refers to the implements of writing as if they were alive: "I can hardly write this—that never to be mentioned without anger—Marie having thrown my beautiful pen *out* of the window on to Dorothea's balcony—consequently producing severe dislocation of the nibs, & general shock to the system, wh. it will probably never entirely get over. After tea read my Roman History, a terrible plough, & talked to dear Dorothea. Nothing to fill up this blank with, & therefore out of consideration to the enfeebled powers of my beloved it shall be left empty—" (June 25). There is humor and high drama in the selection of her writing implements. She dragged Nessa and Adrian to Regent Street "& there with terrible agony & excitement chose a nib for my pen. When we came home I found it was too fine—oh the despair of that moment! So after lunch Nessa & I planned to go & get another one." They returned to Regent Street, "where we boldly demanded another nib, & got this most exquisite and delightful one" (September 24).

The spirit of that description stands apart from the bleakness of all that surrounds it. By the time Virginia wrote it, Stella had died. The mood of the diary now is more characteristically that of an entry dated one month earlier: "Nessa & I walked round & round the tennis lawn after dinner (our custom nowadays) & discussed every thing. It is hopeless & strange." Entries in the diary have become meager. She comments herself on September 14, "Again I forget—This poor diary is lingering on indeed, but death would be shorter & less painful—Never mind, we will follow the year to its end, & then fling diaries & diarising into the corner—to dust & mice & moths & all creeping crawling eating destroying creatures." This is the one place where Virginia endows the diary itself with life—but a life that is precarious indeed, one whose end she will herself hasten.

After Stella's death the journal becomes a bare record, with entries of just a few lines and blank pages with no entry at all. Even pages that are left blank, however, have the date carefully handwritten at the top, so that their blankness appears all the more stark. Virginia registers the sparseness herself: "One day is so like another that I never write about them. Grey cloudy cold days" (132). She is recording the invariable weather of depression.

And then amid the sparseness and the blankness comes a sentence that in its simplicity wrenches the heart. It is easy to read past because of its simplicity, but there is a portentous recognition packed into just a few brief words. The fifteen-year-old girl who has been devouring Carlyle, Macaulay, and other giants of the nineteenth century makes a child's error in a familiar word: "Life is a hard business—one needs a rhinirocerous skin—and that one has not got."

Virginia Woolf never did acquire a rhinirocerous skin. What she came to feel, however, was that her very vulnerability was something to be prized. There is a faint echo, I think, of this simple and astonishing sentence, written when she was fifteen, in a passage that she wrote many years later. In her memoir, she speaks of life's "sledge-hammer blows" and of having the power to "blunt" the force of these blows: "I think this is true, because though I still have the peculiarity that I receive these sudden shocks, they are now always welcome; after the first surprise, I always feel instantly that they are particularly valuable. And so I go on to suppose that *the shock-receiving capacity is what makes me a writer*" (emphasis added). The passage continues:

> I feel that I have had a blow; but it is not, as I thought as a child, simply a blow from an enemy hidden behind the cotton wool of daily life; it is or will become a revelation of some order; it is a token of some real thing behind appearances; and I make it real by putting it into words. It is only by putting it into words that I make it whole; this wholeness means that it has lost its power to hurt me; it gives me, perhaps because by doing so I take away the pain, a great delight to put the severed parts together. Perhaps this is the strongest pleasure known to me. ("A Sketch of the Past," 72)

She wrote these words toward the end of her life. What her adolescent diary reveals is that as early as age fifteen, writing was for Virginia Woolf, as painting was for Lily Briscoe, "the one dependable thing in a world of strife, ruin, chaos."

4

Journals, Ages Seventeen
and Twenty-One

"THE RIGHT USE OF REASON"

A year and a half would go by before Virginia Woolf again took up her pen to keep a journal. When she was seventeen, her family took a seven-week summer holiday in the village of Warboys, in Huntingdonshire (now Cambridgeshire). There they settled into an early-nineteenth-century rectory and spent what Virginia would describe at its end as a "summer [that] ranks among our happiest I think."

At the beginning of the holiday she inscribed on the cover of her diary, in capital letters, "WARBOYS SUMMER HOLIDAYS 1899." Most of the entries are dated, and her intention, it seems, was to write in the journal every day. But before long, gaps of several days begin to appear: this diary follows the usual rhythm of an adolescent diary, taken up and put down again by a young woman who appears less rigid, less frightened than she was at fifteen. And unlike the earlier diary, entries are no longer of uniform length, dutifully filling the space of a page. Some entries go on for pages at a time as she relishes the very act of describing. There are moments of sheer pleasure. On the day the family arrived at Warboys: "The house & garden I cannot describe now; how we snorted the air with our soot sated nostrils, & revelled in the country damp, cool & quiet. Our sensations were so exquisite, so crowded & so jubilant that music alone could keep pace with them or express a tenth part of their vividness" (*A Passionate Apprentice*, 136). And on a rainy day: "It was worth defying authorities had such existed, to feel the cool showers of rain trickling over our cheeks, & to smell the exquisite damp refreshed odours that arose from the road & fields" (157). Yielding to the sensual pleasures of nature, and exuberantly describing the experience, are new to this journal.

But above all, what sets this journal apart from the earlier one is that in its pages Woolf was beginning to practice her art. She was self-conscious and often imitative: some passages are stilted, sprinkled with archaisms: "I own it is a joy to me," "methinks," "I know not how to spell his name." She used this journal to try out other voices on her way to finding her own.

There are entries in which she writes about an experience, then rereads what she has written and comments reflectively not on the experience but on the quality of the writing. The entry for August 7 is one of those that most strongly bears the mark of all she has read, of all the hours in her father's library: "Monotony, so methinks, dwells in these plains. Such melting gray of sky, land & water is the very spirit of monotony. I lay in the punt, which has been padded with rugs & cushions & read a sleepy preaching book; the diary of some ancient Bishop written in flowing ancient English that harmonised with this melancholy melodious monotony (what an awful sentence!) of bank & stream" (138). As a writer, a very well read writer, she aspires to do more than she is able, as yet, to do, and she registers the discrepancy herself:

> Every time I write in this book I find myself drifting into the attractive but impossible task of describing the Fens—till I grow heartily sick of so much feeble word painting; & long for one expressive quotation that should signify in its solitary compass all the glories of earth air & Heaven. Nevertheless I own it is a joy to me to be set down with such a

vast never ending picture to reproduce — reproduction is out of the question — but to gaze at, nibble at & scratch at.

After all we are a world of imitations; all the Arts that is to say imitate as far as they can the one great truth that all can see. Such is the eternal instinct in the human beast, to try & reproduce something of that majesty in paint marble or ink. Somehow ink tonight seems to me the least effectual method of all — & music the nearest to truth. (143)

The grandiloquence of her prose suggests the reach of her ambition.

At one point she reveals that in her mind's eye she is writing not just for herself, but for an imagined reader. She is describing in some detail the procedure for catching moths, an activity in which the four Stephen children collaborated with great enthusiasm:

Sugaring must be explained; briefly, it means that the trees at intervals are smeared with a decoction which is known as sugar, but which contains other ingredients. Rum, & thick black treacle mixed is one prescription & that most often adopted as being independent of the cooks kindness & the kitchens fire; the other is a compound, beer, & treacle (black), boiled up in some obliging kettle that, preferably, has no other vocation. An innocent reader (I suppose a reader sometimes for the sake of variety when I write; it makes me put on my dress clothes such as they are) having got this far still remains in the dark as to the use of such a preparation. This then, is the most scientific way of catching moths. (144)

Having let slip that she is writing in her diary not only for herself but also with an eye to an imagined reader, the young writer seems somewhat embarrassed by what she has revealed: she retreats to a parenthetical explanation that is gently self-deprecatory.

Five days later she offers a humorous account of a garden party given by some Stephen relatives—"a somewhat grim day of pleasure." Again there is implicitly a reader whom she is addressing: "Picture us uncomfortably seated on a towing path; half the party in a ditch, the other half in long grass—a cold wind blowing, with occasional drops of rain." At the end of this entry, which goes on for several pages, she reflects, "This has taken me considerably longer to write than the whole day itself: such a relation of details is extraordinarily difficult, dull & unprofitable to read. However there is no end to writing, & each time I hope that I may make better stuff of it" (149–50).

One of the entries in the journal is an essay that Virginia not only dated but titled and signed. The entry for September 3 is called "A Chapter on Sunsets." To call it a chapter suggests, of course, that she thought of her journal, the record of a summer holiday with her family, as a book. She began the essay immediately after the family had returned from "a sunset expedition," declaring self-consciously, "Nothing methinks is so impossible as to describe a real sunset in pen & ink 3 days after that sunset has faded from the sky." And then, as if she were taking a breath: "To begin then."

Her subject is a sunset and the landscape it illuminates. The elements of the scene, she says, "were three: a red ball of a sun, first; then a low lying bank of gray cloud, whose upper edges were already feathery & fixed to receive into its arms the impetuous descent of the sun god; thirdly, a group of trees which made our horizon; casting their arms against the sky." Her imagery makes it clear that it is a human drama she reads into the landscape. And interestingly, although she began by stating that there were three elements to her scene, she goes on to add another, apparently unwittingly, as if the inclusion of this element had escaped her attention: "then fourthly, a cloud shaped like an angels wing, so—" and here she added a drawing in the margin of the journal, a simple drawing of a triangle, as if the angel's wing she saw in her mind's eye could not be conveyed in words. More interesting still, the cloud's shape reminds her of "some sword of judgment or vengeance," even though, she adds, it had no clearly defined outline.

She describes not only the clouds in the west, where the sun was setting, but the clouds scattered all around the sky. Some were conglomerated in the east and south, "others were sailing like solitary icebergs. All bore on their way the imprint: the dying kiss—of the sun." The metaphor of death appears again in the final sentence of her essay: when they reached home, "no gleams of crimson lived to tell that the sun had sunk."

A sunset is of course a conventional subject. But to choose as the subject of her first essay, one she signed, dated, and titled, the "dying kiss" of the sun and its imprint on the clouds that remain has a particular poignance in the context of Woolf's history of loss. In the midst of this descriptive passage she has penned, upside down on the page, a sentence fragment. Seemingly unrelated to her essay, these three words, in my view, point to the heart of the matter: "Long ago there." Like the shape she drew in the margin of her journal but did not count among the elements of her scene—the angel's wing that is also a sword of judgment or vengeance—the upside-down phrase alludes to a theme that the text excludes, but that is nonetheless charged with meaning. What is fragmentary and marginal in this journal turns out, in fact, to be central.

The content of this journal tells only part of the story. To look at the volume itself, to leaf through it, is to have the impression at times of a chaotic jumble. While there are pages of continuous writing, proceeding sequentially from one sheet to the next, there are also pages on which some of the writing is upside down. There are fragments interspersed in the text, seemingly unrelated to the content of the entry. The backs of some pages are covered with sentence fragments or quotations. Mitchell Leaska (1990), who has superbly edited and annotated Woolf's early journals for publication, has disentangled these fragments from the rest of the text and assembled them as an appendix to the published volume. He takes Woolf at her word and regards the fragments as exercises in penmanship and the trying out of pen nibs. As she declares on the back of the second page,

> This book has now
> This book has now got to be a kind of testing
> ground, where I come to try my new pens. I have
> made the most
> heroic resolution to change my ideas of calligraphy
> in conformance with those of my family, which are
> more
> generally accepted by the world as the correct ones.
> [ink squiggle]
> dear but somewhat too romantic pen
> This This is written with my dear, but somewhat too
> romantic pen.

But we need not take Woolf's declared purpose to have been her only purpose.

The journal she kept at seventeen is on its surface emotionally neutral; it is that of an apprentice writer trying her hand at the description of nature and at writing brief essays. Like the journal she kept at fifteen, it keeps its gaze directed outward. One may learn more about Woolf's inner life by listening to the fragments that cover the backs of some pages or are written upside down and seem to interrupt the text. To assume that these are merely exercises in penmanship would be to ignore the story they tell— through their content, their tone, their juxtapositions, through the very chaos they create on the page.

Perhaps she considered it no more than an exercise in penmanship when she wrote out the beginning lines of a poem upside down on the back of page 17 of her journal. She wrote these lines four more times on the back of page 19, again upside down:

> The woods decay, the woods decay & fall
> The vapours weep their burden to the ground
> Man comes & tills the earth & lies beneath.
> And after many a summer dies the swan.

The poem is Tennyson's "Tithonus." The opening lines of the poem, the lines that she wrote and rewrote, are obviously melancholy in tone: they are about death, death as it comes in the ordinary course of nature, to woods and animals and man alike. But the poem Woolf chose is not simply about the turning of the seasons and the inevitability of death: it is a poem about the *yearning* for death. Aurora, or Eos, goddess of the dawn, loved Tithonus and secured from Zeus eternal life for him. But she had failed to ask for eternal youth, and so he grew older and feebler until at last he begged to be allowed to die. In the final stanza of the poem Tithonus addresses Eos:

> Yet hold me not for ever in thine East:
> How can my nature longer mix with thine?
> Coldly thy rosy shadows bathe me, cold
> Are all thy lights, and cold my wrinkled feet
> Upon thy glimmering thresholds, when the steam

Floats up from those dim fields about the homes
Of happy men that have the power to die,
And grassy barrows of the happier dead.
Release me, and restore me to the ground.

Tithonus contrasts his own state with that of "happy men that
have the power to die," and he begs to be released to join "the
happier dead." The theme of the poem whose opening lines
Woolf wrote and rewrote in her journal at the age of seventeen
is that long life is cruelty. Death is release.

These lines are set apart from the ostensible text of the journal: they are written upside down and appear on the backs of
pages. It is interesting to turn over the pages and see what is written on the front. The entry for August 13, beneath which these
melancholy thoughts appear, is the long, sprightly description of
"Sugaring" and the catching of moths that I quoted earlier. The
writing on the back of the page or upside down constitutes quite
literally a subtext, one whose content and tone are insistently
dark.

On the back of page 9, on August 7, 1899, Virginia wrote the
following, also upside down:

> Long life was not what she wished for. She was
> only glad that there should be some reason for not
> writing.
> She was very happy, & when the long dark winter was
> at an end she said that she was glad to find that the
> day was over in which she had to
>
> Length of life was never looked
> Length

With these fragments in mind, one reads further: five days later,
again on the back of a page, Virginia wrote out another sequence

of fragments. The brief phrase at the beginning of the sequence, which is repeated at the end, seems meaningless in itself. But it declares its meaning when we hear in it an echo of what she had written five days earlier:

Length of

When the wicked man turneth
               when
away from his wickedness
then comes the day of judgment.

When the wicked man
    Turneth away from his
    wrath then comes the
      day of judgment.

When the wicked man
    Turneth away from his
    wrath then comes the day of judgment.
This was hardly to be expected, seeing that neither
she nor her husband were to blame in the matter. But
the whole thing was rather a question of the
extraordinary
good which came from the greatness of Empire.

Length of

This series of fragments begins and ends with a broken-off phrase whose fuller context, appearing pages earlier, alludes to a longing for death. These are fragments, musings, quotations, with abrupt changes of subject and changes of voice. But the theme, the repeated theme, of her fragmentary musings is of guilt and judgment, wrath and blame.

The fragments and quotations that appear upside down and interrupt the text or are written on the backs of pages create an insistent subtext. In contrast with the emotional neutrality of the essays and descriptive pieces, its tone is depressive; its subject, implicitly or explicitly, is often death.

To return to the text itself: One of the more delightful pieces is a description of an evening with the local curate. It is a polished piece of writing, and its author seems rather pleased with it:

> 10 or 11 August
> We had the Curate to dinner last night, which deserves full mention because I have never sat down to a meal with a curate in my life, nor had one, to my knowledge in the house. My interest was awakened in him very easily; I had a dim idea of mythical curates, dwelling in the pages of novels, & receiving satire at the hands of all wielders of Pens —but the fact that a Black Coated gentleman could be a Human Being & not a Hypocrite (outwardly at least—I cannot answer for the condition of the Curate's morals on the strength of one dinner party) was quite strange to me. This young man seems to be largely a person of intelligence with a rather peculiar gift of humorous sarcasm. Occasionally his judgments & stories are bitter; but on the whole, he is merely good humoured & muscular.

And here is the fragment that appears on the back of this page:

> Long ago she had known that there was no longer hope
> for her, but she lived on but she
> Long ago   hope which is said
> Long ago she had known

Happy her
Whose
Happy her

The writing on the back of the page continues but now turns
upside down. And in the context of fragments, there is an astonishingly forthright full sentence:

> There is something that I dare not think of.
> The utmost politeness is
> I am almost certain that the end
> This was not possible of the past
> the past
> they smell sweet

Something that she "dares not think of" intrudes itself nonetheless as the insistent subtext of her journal. The fragments
that underlie and interrupt the text constitute a strong depressive undertow beneath the placid surface of the diary—pulling
toward a past that is irretrievably lost, with tormenting questions
of guilt and blame, and a yearning for death.

The chaos of the journal Woolf kept at seventeen is not only
a matter of her practicing penmanship or trying out pen nibs.
The chaos of her journal is part of the story she was telling.

A final point about the appearance of this diary. In order to
give it a handsome binding, Virginia bought a beautiful leatherbound book. The pages of the diary were torn out of the tablet
in which they were written and glued to the pages of this book,
whose covers thus became the covers for her own. The purchase
of the leatherbound volume, on an expedition to St. Ives, was a
high-spirited occasion, and Virginia describes her achievement
in mock-grandiloquent style: "The work heretofore was con-
tained in one modest paper book, that fronted the world in a
state of nature—naked but not ashamed. Boards it recked not

of, now it boasts boards that amount to the dignity of a binding, being ancient tooled calf—the tooling resplendent today as a hundred years ago" (159).

Opening the leather covers of the diary, the reader encounters first the title page of the published book, a title Virginia copied out again toward the end of the diary. By pasting the pages of her diary onto those of the printed text, she gave each of her own pages a printed heading, so that the title of the volume she bought is reiterated throughout the diary. The leatherbound book that she chose to contain her diary—with its novice exercises in writing, its chaos, its depressive undertow—was Isaac Watt's "LOGICK: or, the Right Use of Reason."

The next journal dates from 1903, when Virginia was twenty-one; letters bridge the four-year period between the journals. At the age of sixteen Virginia had begun a correspondence with her cousin Emma Vaughan. Emma, eight years older, was the daughter of Julia's sister Adeline and her husband Henry Vaughan. Virginia's letters to her cousin are playful and affectionate, filled with fond nicknames: "My Beloved Toad," "My dear and ancient Toad," "My dearest Todkins," "My beloved Todelcranz." It was Emma to whom she wrote about her reluctant social life, as she and Vanessa, coming of age, were pushed, or pulled, into society by their half-brother George, himself the very pink of propriety. This is from a letter she wrote to her cousin at nineteen: "We are failures. Really, we can't shine in Society. I don't know how it's done. We aint popular—we sit in corners and look like mutes who are longing for a funeral. However, there are more important things in this life—from all I hear I shan't be asked to dance in the next, and that is one of the reasons why I hope to go there" (*Letters* 1:43). And it was to Emma that she wrote when their cousin Hervey Fisher "suddenly went worse than ever" and had to be committed to an asylum: "The only thing in this world is music—music and books and one or two pictures. I am going to found a colony where there shall be no marrying—unless you happen to fall in love with a symphony of Beethoven—no human element at all, except what comes through Art—nothing but ideal peace and endless meditation. This world of human beings grows too complicated, my only wonder is that we all don't fill more madhouses: the insane view of life has much to be said for it—perhaps its the sane one after all" (*Letters* 1:41–42). Her commentary on her cousin's madness is a commentary on her own, and on the ways that she herself was able to find peace. The refuge from human complexities, from madness itself, Virginia Woolf wrote at nineteen, is in art—in music, in pictures, in books.

Woolf's letters to Emma continue in a tone of ease and affection into the following year, when there is a sudden and dramatic shift. In April 1902, Leslie Stephen was diagnosed with abdominal cancer. At precisely this time, Virginia began a relationship that would be sustaining to her through her father's long illness and death and through the period beyond. This was a relationship with a woman seventeen years her senior, Violet Dickinson.

Violet Dickinson had been a friend of Stella Duckworth and a frequent visitor to Hyde Park Gate. But it was not until the summer of 1902 that the particular friendship of Virginia and Violet began. "She has taken a great fancy to all the girls," Leslie Stephen observed, "specially to Ginia, who went about with her all day and discoursed upon literary and other matters continuously. Miss Dickinson . . . admires Ginia's intelligence greatly" (Bell 1972, 82). At the time of this visit, Virginia was twenty years old and Violet thirty-seven.

Sir Leslie thought Violet Dickinson a very intelligent woman whose "only fault is that she is 6 feet high." In a playful portrait of Violet that Virginia wrote in 1907—which she typed in violet

ink and bound in violet leather for presentation to her friend[1] —
she, too, makes much of Violet's height. According to this exuberant mock biography, before Violet reached the age of eight she grew to be as tall as the tallest hollyhock in the garden, and she is advised by her aunt, "If you are not to be a Maypole of Derision you must see to it that you shine forth as a Beacon of Godliness."

In her extraordinary physical presence and by temperament, Violet was well suited to be the "lofty and reassuring tower of strength" that she became to her young friend. In the summer of 1902, Virginia recorded her own impressions: she saw Violet as warmhearted and high-spirited, talkative and given easily to laughter, but also as having times of depression and sudden reserves. Virginia concluded that if someone saw Violet only as one of those ladies who are welcome everywhere and not indispensable anywhere, "such an observer would be superficial indeed" (MH/A26, quoted by Bell, 82–83).

The shift in the tone of their friendship is immediately apparent in the correspondence: Virginia's first letter, dated February 1902, begins, "My dear Miss Dickinson." In April, when Sir Leslie's diagnosis was made, she becomes "My dear Violet" in a letter in which Virginia speaks of her apprehensions about her father's health. He had been advised to return from Surrey to consult a doctor in London and warned that surgery might be necessary. By autumn of 1902, Virginia speaks to Violet as an intimate friend; her letters have become warm and playful and tender. "Just count the words in this letter," she wrote in October/November 1902 "and write me as many back, and I like them hot and affectionate." In March 1903, she writes, "Sparroy [Virginia] only flaps her warm blooded paw, and says she has tender

1. The typescript was edited for publication by Hawkes in *Twentieth Century Literature*, 1979, 25:270–302.

memories of a long embrace, in a bedroom. Remember it is my turn for a moveable inside next." And in April: "I have got a double bed—some strange foresight made them give it me—I wish you could come, but I shall see you somehow in London, or your house." And again on July 7, 1903, "It is astonishing what depths—hot volcano depths—your finger has stirred in Sparroy—hitherto entirely quiescent."

Letters over this period glow with a lover's allusions, with a private code for intimacies. Virginia contrasts the calm tone of friendship with the urgency of new love: "Letters are only fit for friendship. Intimacy ought to take to telegraphs." These letters are charged with passion, but they are also filled with tender concern and longing. Facing her father's illness and anticipating, ultimately, his death, Virginia turned to Violet Dickinson as the mother she yearned for, the mother from whom she need never be separated: "I wish you were a Kangeroo and had a pouch for small Kangeroos to creep to" (June 4, 1903). The tender image of Violet as mother recurs unabashedly throughout this correspondence, Virginia portraying herself as a small creature, often a sparrow, one of her favorite nicknames for herself in her relationship to Violet: "What a wonderful woman you are for harbouring colds. Take the Sparroy to your breast instead! Father has had rather a bad tired day, after a restless night, but they dont seem to think anything of it. . . . I dont see any reason why this delightful letter should ever stop. I like drivelling away, as a Baby slobbers, to my Violet" (October/November 1903). And again, "Such a brilliant woman as you are . . . ought to be happy—all her friends cawing with open beaks for her to feed them—Sparroy widest agape of all" (November 27, 1903).

But the tenderness and protectiveness she sought Virginia also reciprocated. In a letter written in June 1903, she expresses concern about Violet's back, which had been hurt. Here she uses for the first time an image she would use again in an important passage of the memoir she wrote toward the end of her life: "Fate," she wrote to Violet at twenty-one, "is a brutal sledge hammer, missing all the people she might knock on the head, and crashing into the midst of such sensitive and exquisite creatures as my Violet. I wish I could shield you with my gross corpse" (June 1903).

There would be further sledgehammer blows for Woolf herself. Her father underwent surgery in December 1902; by April 1903, his condition had grown worse. In November 1903 he dictated to Virginia the final part of the memoir that he had begun just after the death of her mother.[2] By December 1903, Virginia's letters to Violet become almost daily bulletins about her father's decline. Their singleness of focus makes it unnecessary to say, at the beginning of a letter, whom the pronoun "he" refers to: "My Violet, He seems very weak today," "My Violet, He is about the same," "My Violet, His temp. is 100, but they say this doesn't count much. He is very weak, and Heaven knows what is going to happen. It can't go on like this much longer."

Of her reliance on Violet, "firm as a lighthouse above it all," Virginia wrote, "Its peace and balm to talk to you and that is the only kind of good there is in the world. . . . You are a beloved creature—*that* is what I wanted to say—and it makes it all different to have you."

Anticipating the death of her father, Woolf had the sudden impulse to save Violet's letters as a way to preserve their relationship: "My Beloved Woman, Your letters come like balm on

2. One may hear an echo of the ending of Sir Leslie's memoir in Virginia's suicide note. His penultimate sentence reads, "I have only to say to you, my children, that you have all been as good and tender to me as anyone could be during these last months and indeed years." In the letter she left for her husband to read after her death Virginia wrote, "All I want to say is that until this disease came on we were perfectly happy. . . . No one could have been so good as you have been, from the first day till now."

the heart. I really think I must do what I never have done—try to keep them. I've never kept a single letter all my life—but this romantic friendship ought to be preserved" (May, 4, 1903). As indeed it is.

We turn to the journal of 1903 knowing from these letters what a harrowing year this was, as Virginia watched her father's slow decline. If the journal of 1899 had been that of a seventeen-year-old girl beginning to practice her art, the journal of 1903 is that of a young woman of twenty-one who defines herself as a writer: "As an artist fills his pages with scraps & fragments, studies of drapery—legs, arms & noses—useful to him no doubt, but of no meaning to anyone else—so I take up my pen & trace here whatever shapes I happen to have in my head" (*A Passionate Apprentice*, 186–87). The earlier journal had one entry that she titled and signed; that of 1903, although she called it a diary, was conceived explicitly as a book. At the beginning she has carefully compiled an "Index," a complete listing of the contents and the page number on which each essay begins. Five of the essays, indeed, are uncertain in their dating because she sent them first to Violet Dickinson for her criticism and only afterward copied them into the diary.

Woolf regarded the diary of 1903 as a sort of sketchbook in which to trace "whatever shapes I happen to have in my head." What were these shapes? The titles of the essays listed in her Index indicate the subjects that served her: the diary begins and ends in London, but most of the pieces were written on a family holiday, this one near Salisbury. Many are descriptions of excursions she took with members of her family: "An Expedition to Hampton Court," "Netherhampton House," "Stonehenge," "Romsey Abbey," "Stonehenge Again." Others are exercises in description: "The Water Meadows," "The Downs," "The Storm." Still others are brief essays: "Thoughts upon Social Success," "The Talk of Sheep," "Country Reading." And here, for the first time, the future novelist tries her hand at the description of character, in a sketch of her Greek tutor, Janet Case. Letters from this period document, day by day, her father's slow decline and her own anguish, but the essays, in their subject matter and tone, give no hint of what is beneath their reflective surface.

And then, at the end of the journal, is an essay chilling in its portentousness. The piece is entitled "The Serpentine," named for the narrow, curling lake across Hyde Park. The subject is a brief item that caught her eye in the newspaper: the body of a woman who committed suicide by drowning has been found. One reads this entry knowing that despite the calm surface of the essays in this journal, Virginia was helplessly watching, day by day, her father's approaching death. We read the essay, moreover, written when she was twenty-one, knowing that at the age of fifty-nine she herself would commit suicide in the same way as the anonymous woman whose body was pulled from the Serpentine.

She begins her essay in a tone of ironic detachment. Noting that "the evening paper is always prolific in tragedies," she comments that "the average number of husbands have murdered their wives while in drink or out of it, & love sick shop girls & maniacs have rushed to their knives & poison pots with unusual frequency." But she cannot sustain her distance. She literally makes the story her own. She fleshes out the bare bones of the newspaper account, filling in particulars where none have been given. Here, in its entirety, is the item that appeared in the *Evening News and Evening Mail* on September 23, 1903:

> PATHETIC LETTER. No evidence of identification was offered at the Westminster Coroner's court this forenoon, in the case of the woman whose dead body

was found floating in the Serpentine. The woman was poorly dressed, and her hat, shoes, and stockings were found hanging on the rails near the Serpentine. The only articles found on her were a small pencil and a piece of paper on which was written: "No father, no mother, no work. I do hope the Lord will help me. I do hope to be forgiven for what I have done." (*A Passionate Apprentice*, 211)

That is all the information provided in the newspaper account. And here is what Woolf's imagination made of it:

She was quite dead, & there was nothing to be done but take her to the mortuary & leave her for her relations to identify. Her soaked clothes were taken off, & the pockets searched in case her name or address might be found there. Very few people go out of the world in silence; almost every dead man or woman who is picked up has written some word of apology or farewell or justification. The most friendless knows that some one—if only the coroner—will be curious to learn what drove him to this last step— and it was so in this case. A scrap of paper was found pinned to the inside of her dress as though she had meant to keep it from the water as long as possible. It was blurred but the writing was still legible. Her last message to the world—whatever its import, was short—so short that I can remember it. "No father, no mother, no work" she had written "May God forgive me for what I have done tonight." (212)

The taking off of her soaked clothes, the searching of her pockets, the note pinned to the inside of her dress to keep it from the water for as long as possible, the writing now blurred by water but still legible—all come from Woolf's imagination, not the newspaper.

She imagines herself into the mind of this stranger, attributing to the drowned woman a determination that is recognizably that of a writer—a determination that the words she wrote be read. The woman's intentionality—the pinning of her suicide note to the inside of her dress "as though *she had meant* to keep it from the water" (the phrase that emphasizes her purposefulness was added in a revision)—is wholly Woolf's creation. Through projective identification she brings the dead woman to life; she imagines the reasons for an unknown woman to take her own life in precisely the way that she herself ultimately would do:

> I could not get the words out of my head. "No father, no mother, no work," & so she killed herself. Had this been the act & writing of a girl it would have been sad enough—but that a woman of 45 should have written this for testament struck me as infinitely sadder. She had had her trial in life, time enough in 45 years to make test of all human relationships—daughterhood, wifehood, motherhood. Whether she knew these two last we cannot say— happiest for her if she had never known them—for last night she counted them as nothing. It was for her father & mother that this middle aged woman yearned—a father & mother, maybe, who died when she was a child. (212)

She has supplied an age for the woman and imagines a life story for her, a life story that, like her own, is one of repeated loss: "She became a wife without thought of her parents, & a mother with hardly any memory of her own mother. But her husband leaves her for some other woman, & her children die, or desert her. Then of a sudden comes that pang—Without husband or children, I yet had my parents. If they were alive now I should not be alone. Whatever my sin my father & mother would have given me protection & comfort. For the first time in her life perhaps she weeps for her parents & for the first time knows all that they were, & her loneliness without them" (212). In conjuring up the woman's sense of abandonment and her belated grief for the parents who died when she was a child, Woolf has lost whatever distance remained between herself and her subject. She has slipped into the first person and into the present tense.

Her own life history had convinced her that the death of a parent is life's most irreparable loss, "one that nothing can heal & no fresh tie renew. Your husband may die & you can marry another—your children may die & others may be born to you, but if your father & mother die you have lost something that the longest life can never bring again" (212–13). This is the cry of a child who has already lost her mother and is facing the imminent death of her father, who could imagine no other ties in life as sustaining as these.

But there was more to the anonymous woman's brief note: "No father, no mother, no work" she had written, and Woolf was arrested, too, by the last of these terms:

> But there was one thing left which might make life endurable . . . that was work. I do not believe that she coupled this word with the sacred names of father & mother in any merely material sense—by work she meant bread & butter, but she also meant something nobler. She had learnt perhaps the self respect & purity that come from work, & the blessed peace with which it deadens sorrow. Before she died then she would try to find work. . . . At any rate she found no work, as one may read in the bitter line

which water cannot efface "No father, no mother, no work." (213)

Woolf imagines the woman's lack of work not only as an economic misfortune—as undoubtedly it was to a woman who would be buried in a pauper's grave—but as a psychic misfortune. Whatever work may have been for the anonymous woman who drowned herself in the Serpentine in September 1903, for Woolf herself it was at this time—and would be throughout her life—the most reliable way she had to deaden sorrow. She imagines for the stranger the final peace that she herself would ultimately seek: "Then slipping off the weight that had been too much for her, she sank in the waters. Whoever she is that sleeps tonight in a grave without a name, may she sleep well, as surely the tired have right to sleep" (213). In the manuscript a word has been crossed out: at first the dead woman slept not in a "grave" without a name, but in a "home" without a name.

5

Early Reviews and Essays

AGE TWENTY-TWO TO TWENTY-THREE

While Virginia Woolf was writing her meditation on suicide, her father was declining visibly, the ebbing of his strength documented day by day in her letters. "If he had died at first it would have been easier," she wrote to Violet Dickinson on the last night of the year 1903, "but now one has to give up more—I mean all these days he has been there, and able to talk a little, and one has had time to think—however, I know I shall be glad for him." Still Leslie Stephen lingered on, into February of the new year. Through this protracted period of suffering, her father's and her own, Virginia found refuge as she had always done: "Life, I am sure, is no pleasure to him—and he would have been glad to die a week ago—but theres no help for it. It is so hard to wait and see him get slowly weaker day by day. But these are the things one has to go through in this Brute of a world apparently. . . . Books are such a mercy" (February 1904).

Her twenty-second birthday fell during the last weeks of her father's life. On that day, January 25, 1904, she wrote to Violet, "Father gave me a ring—really a beautiful one, which I love— the first ring I have ever had. This time even, has compensations. It amazes me how much I get out of my Father, still— and he says I am a very good daughter! He is the most delightful of people—and Lord knows how we shall ever get along alone." His long illness and the imminence of his death obliterated, for now, her deep ambivalence, revising her sense of the past: "But we have all been so happy together and there never was anybody so loveable."

Finally, at 7 A.M. on February 22, 1904, Leslie Stephen died. "How to go on without him, I dont know," she wrote to Janet Case the next day. "All these years we have hardly been apart, and I want him every moment of the day. But we still have each other—Nessa and Thoby and Adrian and I, and when we are together he and Mother do not seem far off."

A few days after the funeral, Vanessa, Thoby, Adrian, and Virginia, accompanied by George Duckworth, went for a month to Manorbier, on the Pembrokeshire coast. Letters from Manorbier express her yearning for her father and a poignant disbelief: "Oh dear, what a world it is! I keep thinking I shall find Father at home—and what I shall tell him—" (March 1904). More ominously, they begin to dwell upon her guilt and remorse, not unlike that of her father after the death of her mother: "The dreadful thing is that I never did enough for him all those years. He was so lonely often, and I never helped him as I might have done. This is the worst part of it now. If he had only lived we could have been so happy. But it is all gone" (February 28, 1904). Again: "I cant believe that all our life with Father is over and he dead. If one could only tell him how one cared, as I dreamt I did last night" (March 1904). And again: "If he had only lived I could have made up. I think he just knew how much I cared, and the happy time was just beginning—and now it is all over. That is what seems so cruel. If I could only tell him once—" (March 31, 1904).

The tributes to Sir Leslie seemed to her woefully inadequate and angered her: "Stupid fools! I could have written them better." Obituaries made her father seem distant, when what she wanted most was to feel his presence: "All this stupid writing and reading about father seems to put him further away, only I know nothing can do that, and I have the curious feeling of living with him every day. I often wonder as we sit talking what it is I am waiting for, and then I know I want to hear what he thinks. It was a most exquisite feeling to be with him, even to touch his hand—he was so quick, and that one finds in no one else" (March 4, 1904).

Later that year, looking back on the month at Manorbier, Woolf reflected on the way her writing had served her at this time: "I was writing then to prove to myself that there was nothing wrong with me—which I was already beginning to fear there was" (November 10, 1904).

After returning home, the four Stephens, accompanied by Gerald Duckworth, spent the months of April and May in Venice, Florence, and Paris. Toward the end of this trip, Virginia had an increasing sense that something was wrong. As a bulwark against danger, characteristically she thought most urgently of work: "Oh Lord, how cross I have been, how dull, how tempersome,—and am still . . . Oh my Violet if you could only find me a great solid bit of work to do when I get back that will make me forget my own stupidity I should be so grateful. I *must* work" (May 6, 1904). The urgency of her plea, written within three months of her father's death, recalls the meditation on suicide that she wrote as his death approached and the brief note of the anonymous woman that had seized Virginia's imagination: "No father, no mother, no work." She herself now had no father and no mother, and she knew in her bones that work would be essential for her own survival.

On May 10, the day after the family's return from Paris, Virginia had a severe breakdown. For three months she remained at Violet Dickinson's house at Welwyn, where she required the care of three nurses, toward whom she became violent at times. Here she made her first suicide attempt, throwing herself from a window (one that, according to Quentin Bell [1972], was not so high that the fall could cause her serious harm). Other symptoms were unequivocal in their ominousness: "She heard voices urging her to acts of folly; she believed that they came from overeating and that she must starve herself. . . . She lay in bed, listening to the birds singing in Greek and imagining that King Edward VII lurked in the azaleas using the foulest language possible. All that summer she was mad" (Bell, 89–90).

There are no letters, no diaries from that summer. The next time we hear the voice of Virginia Woolf herself it is September 1904. By now she was thought well enough to join her family on holiday in Nottinghamshire, accompanied by Nurse Traill. In a letter to Violet she looks back on that terrible summer and reflects upon her delusions, still not fully disbelieving them:

> You will be glad to hear that your Sparroy feels herself a recovered bird. I think the blood has really been getting into my brain at last. It is the oddest feeling, as though a dead part of me were coming to life. I cant tell you how delightful it is—and I dont mind how much I eat to keep it going. All the voices I used to hear telling me to do all kinds of wild things have gone—and Nessa says they were always only my imagination. They used to drive me nearly mad at Welwyn, and I thought they came from overeating—but they cant, as I still stuff and they are gone. (September 22(?), 1904)

Though clearly she feels herself to be out of the woods, she is not yet altogether sure about the unreality of the voices she heard: she needs to bring in the authority of Nessa to bolster her conviction. And she still needs to marshall evidence to show that the voices she heard could not have come from overeating: she eats abundantly now, yet she no longer hears those voices.

But overall the tone of her letters is that of someone who has returned to life: "Oh my Violet, if there were a God I should bless him for having delivered me safe and sound from the miseries of the last six months! You cant think what an exquisite joy every minute of my life is to me now, and my only prayer is that I may live to be 70. . . . I can never tell you what you have been to me all this time—for one thing you wouldn't believe it—but if affection is worth anything you have, and always will have, mine" (September 26, 1904). The letter ends with an important postscript: "I am longing to begin work." She repeats these words a few days later, sounding the theme that would be central to her recovery: "I am longing to begin work. I know I can write, and one of these days I mean to produce a good book. What do you think? Life interests me intensely, and writing is I know my natural means of expression" (September 30, 1904).

The urgency she felt about beginning to work soon found its focus. F. W. Maitland, her father's biographer and a family friend, asked her to read through her parents' letters to each other, to select and copy out those that would be appropriate for the *Life* of Sir Leslie that he was writing. It is in a letter to Violet that Virginia first ventures the thought of doing more: "I am going to see Fred Maitland on Monday, which I very much want to do. I feel as though I could write something worth adding or quoting, to the Life. But he is perfectly capable of understanding everything" (October 22, 1904). Over the following days she warmed to her task: "I am getting through my copying—and now I have to go through 2 vols: of extracts from Father's and mother's letters to each other. They are so private that Fred wont look at them himself, and I have to decide what he ought to see and possibly publish. I am very anxious to get on and write something, very short of course, which Fred can read and get a hint from or possibly quote from" (October 30, 1904). Each time she refers to the idea of writing about her father, the thought is cloaked in diffidence, yet the letters make clear how essential this project was in helping her to recover from the psychotic state into which she was plunged by his death.

The same letter makes another momentous proposal, phrased

in a way that makes it easy to read past: "Would Mrs Lyttelton like a description of a Q.(uaker) Meeting from my gifted pen, d'you think. I dont know if I shall have time, but it might be amusing." Mrs. Lyttelton, who was a friend of Violet Dickinson, was the editor of the Women's Supplement of *The Guardian,* a London weekly newspaper for clerical readers. This inquiry about Mrs. Lyttelton, feigning an offhand tone, marks the beginning of Virginia Woolf's career as a writer.

The letter was written from Cambridge, where Virginia was staying for a month with her Quaker aunt, Caroline Emilia, while Vanessa organized the move of the four Stephens from their childhood home, 22 Hyde Park Gate, to Bloomsbury. Virginia's stay in Cambridge was considered part of her recuperation, but in her view it meant exile from what was most dear:

> London means my own home, and books, and pictures, and music, from all of which I have been parted since February now, — and I have never spent such a wretched 8 months in my life. And yet that tyrannical, and as I think, shortsighted Savage[1] insists upon another two. . . . I long for a large room to myself, with books and nothing else, where I can shut myself up, and see no one, and read myself into peace. . . .
>
> Really a doctor is worse than a husband! Oh how thankful I shall be to be my own mistress and throw their silly medicines down the slop pail! I never shall believe, or have believed, in anything any doctor says

---

1. Dr. George Savage, later Sir George, was an old friend of the family. In the course of his career he was physician-superintendent of the Bethlehem Royal Hospital, president of the Medico-Psychological Association of Great Britain, and examiner in mental physiology, University of London.

—I learnt their utter helplessness when Father was ill. They can guess at what's the matter, but they cant put it right. (October 30, 1904)

Doctors had been helpless against her father's illness, as they had been against her mother's and Stella's; and they were helpless too against her own. "Read myself into peace": the phrase from this letter she wrote at twenty-two might have come from her diary at fifteen. In the face of life's blows, what had proved most soothing and sustaining, always, were books.

In a letter to her cousin Emma, she looks back to the "terrible afternoon" of May 10, when her acute breakdown began. Emma had come to borrow some letters, she recalls: "I was hardly knowing what I did or said, and wondered if you noticed it. Well, for at least three months after that, I was more or less incapable of doing anything but eat and sleep, and had to be watched by three fiends of nurses. However, thank Heaven, that nightmare has dispersed at last: only Savage says I must live . . . the life of a valetudinarian for the next year. . . . I have to spend the next two months out of London—and as Gordon Square is ready and lovely, full of books and pictures, my language is not measured" (November 1, 1904). This letter, which has her aunt Caroline Emilia's Cambridge address in Virginia's hand in the upper right corner, is written on stationery that has printed at the top the Stephens' new London address: 46 Gordon Square.

When Virginia joined her sister and brothers there, she found an astute gift from Violet waiting for her: "When I came into my room, the first thing I saw was your lovely and most satisfactory and exactly what I had thought of inkpot, with all his holes, and a well for ink deep enough to write a dozen articles for the Guardian" (November 8, 1904).

Over the next weeks Virginia's letters to Violet are sprinkled with references to Mrs. Lyttelton and the *Guardian*, their tone a mixture of nervousness and eagerness, self-doubt and bragga-docio. Sending Violet an essay she had written at Manorbier, she says, "I think I may as well send this to Mrs Lyttelton to show her the kind of thing I do. Of course I dont for a moment expect her to take *this* which is probably too long or too short, or in some way utterly unsuitable" (November 10, 1904). Again the following day,

> I dont in the least expect Mrs Lyttelton to take that article—I stupidly didn't typewrite it—indeed wrote it myself rather hurriedly and illegibly as I hate copying—and forgot to give my address, or to enclose a stamped envelope for return. So I dont think my chances are good. I dont in the least want Mrs L's candid criticism; I want her cheque! I know all about my merits and failings better than she can from the sight of one article, but it would be a great relief to know that I could make a few pence easily in this way. . . . I honestly think I can write better stuff than that wretched article you sent me. Why on earth does she take such trash?—But there is a knack of writing for newspapers which has to be learnt, and is quite independent of literary merits.
>
> So I dont much care if she does say my writing wont do. . . . My hope is that she will say she would like to see other things. I could easily re-write some old things, or write new ones, if I have time. (November 11, 1904)

And three days later: "D'you think Mrs. Lyttelton will let me write fairly often?—and what does she pay for these little arti-cles? Not much, I suppose—indeed they aren't worth much—and I cant conceive why she has them. Would she let me review ever?"

Toward the end of November, Mrs. Lyttelton sent her William Dean Howells's novel *The Son of Royal Langbrith,* and Woolf's review appeared in the *Guardian* of December 14, 1904. It was her first work to be published. And on December 21 it was followed by an essay on Haworth Parsonage.

Now settled in London, she wrote to her cousin Madge Vaughan, "I wish you could see my room at this moment, on a dark winter's evening—all my beloved leather backed books standing up so handsome in their shelves, and a nice fire, and the electric light burning, and a huge mass of manuscripts and letters and proof-sheets and pens and inks over the floor and everywhere" (*Letters* 1:167). It is a scene of coziness and abundance and safety, as Virginia Woolf, at twenty-two, begins her career as a writer.

The year 1904, which ended in this tableau of well-being, with the happy helter-skelter of books and the implements of writing, had begun with the death of her father, followed by her own descent for months into the nightmare world of psychosis. With the beginning of the new year, 1905, she again began to keep a journal. In early February she wrote with relief and pleasure of returning to her studies: "This is the first Greek I have done since my illness—since February, that is—almost a year ago. I remember the last morning's work at Thucydides, and how my brain felt sucked up. I am glad to find that I don't forget Greek and read Thucydides which is tough, as easily as I ever did" (*A Passionate Apprentice,* 231). Similarly two weeks later: "There is a charm in Latin, which haunts one. Even that little bit of Virgil with Thoby in the summer, when I was hardly able to use my brains, brought a sense of harmony into them, such as for many months they had not known" (238). In Greek, in Latin—in the exercise of her mind—she could find the closest thing to refuge from the chaos of madness.

As she began to submit articles for publication, her letters to Violet reflect a mix of apprehension and excitement: "I cant think why you condemn me to suffer so needlessly. Mightn't you have saved me 2 *sleepless* nights—if not 3—by telling me straight out *what* Mr Haldane said of Haworth? . . . Now, also, in your next letter written immediately on getting this, tell me if Mrs. Lyttelton thought me impertinent for telling her to do what she liked with my articles" (December 30, 1904). And again,

> I am so cross today, crosser than ever—that fool of a man, the Cornhill editor, sends me back my Article—Boswells letters—without a word, but a printed slip. I never expected him to take it, since I found that it would only make 2 Cornhill pages which is impossibly short of course—but I thought he might say so. Also Haldane isnt exactly warm in his praise, and altogether I feel, as you read in the Bible, despised and rejected of men. . . .
>
> I shall be rather—in fact very—glad to be home, in my own room, with my books, and I want to work like a steam engine, though editors wont take what I write. I must show you what I have done, when it is typed, and please be very kind. (early January 1905)

Near the beginning of 1905, she records in her journal a significant event: "Found this morning on my plate my first installment of wages—£2.7.6 for the Guardian articles, which gave me great pleasure." As the year went on, she felt increasing pride and dignity in "making a living, as I do, by the pen."

She boasted in a letter to her cousin Emma Vaughan that

> I am realising the ambition of our youth, and actually making money—which, however, I spend

long before I make. I am writing for—now for my
boast—
The Times Lit. Supplement.
The Academy
The National Review
The Guardian—
Aint that respectable. My National Review article is about [Street] *Music* so you can imagine what
a flutter is going through the musical world—it has
probably reached Dresden [where Emma had been
studying music]. My remarks will revolutionise the
whole future of music. (February 23, 1905)

The date of this high-spirited letter is noteworthy: the previous
day was the first anniversary of her father's death. It had been a
remarkable twelve months.

A few days later, in a letter to Violet, Virginia copied out
verbatim Fred Maitland's response to what she wrote about her
father for the *Life*. ("Beautiful. Really it is beautiful. . . . I can
only say that what you write is just what your Father would have
wished you to write.") Having repeated his praise with obvious
pride, she then claims that she does not want what she has written to be published. Later, as a compromise, her piece was signed
"by one of his daughters." The alternation of pride and anxiety,
ambition and diffidence, runs through the letters written during
these early months of her career.

Letters to Violet, which earlier had been bulletins on her father's slow decline, are now bulletins on the progress of her
work. Day by day they record the praise or criticism she receives,
the new assignments coming in, the fluctuations in her confidence: "I have been toiling at a beast of a review all the morning, which I cant write and hate writing and write d——d badly.
By the way I was in Fridays Times, and Bruce Richmond [edi-

tor] thought it 'admirable' and now sends me another great, fat book—which I dont much want to do—as I know *nothing* of the subject. I despair of my brains, which seem to be guttering like a tallow candle" (March 11, 1905).

Letters to Violet have little of the erotic aura they had had—the teasing tone of lovers, the allusions to private jokes. Now Virginia turns to her warmly and gratefully and with sufficient trust to confide her self-doubt and her need for reassurance: "Do you really think it good enough to send—because I needn't?" (*Letters* 1:191). "I wish I had you here to encourage. No one really takes very much interest, why should they, in my scribblings. Do you think I shall ever write a really good book?" (*Letters* 1:208). Always she was sensitive to criticism and to praise: "Kitty writes that she has made great friends with the writer of Elizabeth's German Garden; who says, what is the point of the story, that *my* article on *Music* interested her so much!!!" (190). It is a sensitivity she would retain throughout her life to a degree that was sometimes crippling; here, there is a charming girlishness to the triple exclamation points, the italics, the unabashed boast.

But for all the girlishness of the letters, the published pieces speak with authority. There is confidence in her judgments and a felicitous rhythm to her prose. Virginia Woolf reviews books as one writer evaluating the art of another. In one of her earliest pieces she takes on Henry James. The novel is *The Golden Bowl:*

> For all the skill and care that have been spent on them the actors remain but so many distinguished ghosts. We have been living with thoughts and emotions, not with live people. The effect of all this marvellous accumulation of detail—all of it doubtless true, all there to see if we look close enough—obscures the main outlines. Mr. James is like an artist who, with a sure knowledge of anatomy, paints every

bone and muscle in the human frame; the portrait would be greater as a work of art if he were content to say less and suggest more. (*Essays* 1:23)

She resented the fact that her review was cut by the editors and protested to Violet that now it was worthless and did not represent all the work she had put into it. The book, she said, deserved "a good and careful" review. These are not the virtues of the one she wrote: her own, at the beginning of her career, was bold and audacious.

Among these early pieces, some remain fresh and vital even when the works she is reviewing have long been forgotten. In writing about books by women and books about women, Woolf begins to sound themes she would amplify more than twenty years later in *A Room of One's Own*. An example is her review of a novel called *Nancy Stair*, by Elinor MacCartney Lane. It is set in the eighteenth century. The heroine, who is motherless, has a father who recognizes his daughter's gifts and is determined to give her a man's education. Talented and educated, she grows up to become a famous poet but chooses to turn her back on poetry when she falls in love:

> She realises "how little value verse-making holds to the real task of living," and understands the real task of living to mean, for a woman at any rate, marriage and motherhood. The genius for poetry seems to be incompatible with the duties of wife and mother, and, as the least important, Nancy has no hesitation in quenching it in order to marry and live happily ever afterwards. This is the eighteenth-century solution of the doubts of the nineteenth century. Such a solution is, of course, the popular one, and it is right, perhaps, that a novelist should take a sentimental point of view and rejoice at the conven-

tional ending. The prosaic mind may be tempted to suggest that the world might, perhaps, be considerably poorer if the great writers had exchanged their books for children of flesh and blood. (*Essays* 1:40)

In the end she relents and halfheartedly credits the author with having written a lively story. Often reviews that are critical end with a final sentence beginning "But . . ." followed by some words of praise. Perhaps it was this sort of undoing that led Woolf, later, to look back on her early writing as showing too much her training at the tea table. But while she may have thought the sharpness of her point softened here—by the words "may," "tempted," "suggest," "perhaps"—it is surely not dulled. These early writings are remarkable less for a "ladylike" quality she would later regret than for the strength and confidence of her judgments.

In a review that appeared in the *Guardian* on January 25, 1905 (her twenty-third birthday), Woolf took on an author who was a philosopher, journalist, and sometime fellow of New College, Oxford. The book, by William Leonard Courtney, is called *The Feminine Note in Fiction:*

> Women, we gather, are seldom artists, because they have a passion for detail which conflicts with the proper artistic proportion of their work. We would cite Sappho and Jane Austen as examples of two great women who combine exquisite detail with a supreme sense of artistic proportion. Women, again, excel in "close analytic miniature work;" they are more happy when they reproduce than when they create; their genius is for psychological analysis—all of which we note with interest, though we reserve our judgment for the next hundred years. (*Essays* 1:16)

After summarizing Courtney's patronizing clichés about the nature of women, the review ends, "Is it not too soon after all to criticise the 'feminine note' in anything? And will not the adequate critic of women be a woman?"

This early work shows Woolf's mastery over the rhetorical power of understatement and irony, a gift she would display to some effect in *A Room of One's Own*. She did not choose the books she reviewed; she reviewed what was sent to her. And the early reviews were unsigned. But her particular alertnesses mark the reviews as her own. She bristled at stereotypes about women's writing and at the suggestion that the traditional role of women was more estimable than that of the writer. And she wrote compellingly about the way in which women who fulfill this traditional role, even those who are thought to do so beautifully, are lost to history, lost, indeed, to memory.

Writing about a book entitled *Some Famous Women of Wit and Beauty: A Georgian Galaxy*, she observes that present-day readers find it difficult to account, fifty years later, for the power these women had in the eyes of their contemporaries. "The secret of the spell seems to have died in each case with its possessor. . . . If it survives the grave at all, it is as some phantom and elusive will-o-the-wisp, which flits through the vague region of Victorian memoir-writers and leaves us with empty hands when we try to grasp it" (61). The metaphor recalls her own attempts, in her memoir, to take hold of her mother in memory, and how elusive she found her to be.

After the death of Julia Stephen, Sir Leslie would ask repeatedly to be reassured that as a husband he had not been as bad as Carlyle, had he? Thomas Carlyle was emblematic of the man of genius who was voracious in his needs, and Jane Welsh Carlyle a brilliant woman who spent herself in serving those needs. Married to a formidable man whose demands could fully absorb the energies of his wife, Jane Carlyle was worn down by the exigencies of the task: it was a theme that was resonant in the Stephen household. In her first year as journalist Woolf published an article in the *Guardian* on "The Letters of Jane Carlyle." In its artfulness it is one of those early essays that continue to reward the reader:

> Few people, indeed, have been able to cast so brilliant an image of themselves upon paper. And yet it is noteworthy that she has not taken advantage of the usual method of self-portraiture that recommends itself to letter-writers; she seldom talks of herself as other than an active and practical human being. Letters of the "inner woman" sort, "all about feelings," anything that savoured of self-analysis or introspection she checked ruthlessly. But in spite of this reserve, which drove her to make her letters out of facts, they were facts which did more to illuminate herself than most people's feelings. (*Essays* 1:54)

In concluding the article, Woolf says of this woman who "had to give up her ambition to work with her pen" that "she might sometimes resent the fate which had driven her to squander all her gifts on such apparently trivial ends—'the eternal writing of little unavoidable notes' and the rest—but that is not a reflection that will occur to her readers. Under other conditions she might have written more; she could hardly have written better."

The emotion she attributes to Jane Carlyle herself is tempered: it is not rage but "resentment" that she "might" and only "sometimes" feel about the "apparent" triviality of her ends. Moreover, Woolf claims that such a reflection will not occur to Jane Carlyle's readers—even as she ensures that such a reflection *must* occur to her readers. The gentleness she ascribes to

Jane Carlyle is undercut by the tone of Woolf's own voice. Jane Welsh Carlyle "squandered" all her gifts: the verb Woolf chooses is fierce in its indignation. This essay stands as a tribute to a woman whose gifts were lost to history, "squandered" as they were on the endless trivial demands of a woman's life. (Of this highly accomplished piece, Virginia wrote nervously to Violet, "I have been sent the proof of Mrs. Carlyle. O Lord it is bad—such an ugly angular piece of writing, all jagged edges. Do you feel convinced I *can* write?" [*Letters* 1:202]).

The marriage of the Carlyles—and its effect on Jane Carlyle—is a subject to which Woolf would return. In 1909, writing about their letters to one another in the years before their marriage ("More Carlyle Letters") she observed that "the letters which began so respectfully with talk of her genius and future became more and more occupied with his own" (*Essays* 1:260). Fifteen years later, in the essay "Character in Fiction" her language is no longer tempered: "Consider the married life of the Carlyles, and bewail the waste, the futility, for him and for her, of the horrible domestic tradition which made it seemly for a woman of genius to spend her time chasing beetles, scouring saucepans, instead of writing books" (*Essays* 3:422).[2]

That there are indeed "other conditions" under which a woman like Jane Welsh Carlyle need not have given up "her ambition to work with her pen" are matters that Woolf would take up, brilliantly, in *A Room of One's Own*. In her early reviews and essays, she not only anticipated its themes, she exemplified its famous dictum: "We think back through our mothers if we are women." The mothers she thought back through were women like Jane Carlyle, who gave up her ambition to work with her pen but wrote letters that shimmer with the intelligence she squan-

2. See also "Geraldine and Jane" in *The Second Common Reader.*

dered; women whose writings were patronized by their male critics; women of wit and beauty who were compelling to their contemporaries, but whose "spell seems to have died in each case with its possessor." There is only one way for such women to survive the grave: "Genius alone can preserve for us the wit that has been spoken and the beauty that has long faded, by creating them afresh."

At the beginning of her career as a writer, Woolf asserted the primacy of the imagination over the so-called real world. In a review called "Literary Geography" she discusses two books about the country of Dickens and Thackeray, books that set out to describe the places in which these writers lived and which they wrote about. Innocuous enough, seemingly, but Woolf dismisses the enterprise. "A writer's country," she argues, "is a territory within his own brain." This territory is more real than brick and mortar: "No city indeed is so real as this that we make for ourselves and people to our liking; and to insist that it has any counterpart in the cities of the earth is to rob it of half its charm. In the same way too the great dead come to each of us in their own guise, and their image is more palpable and enduring than any shapes of flesh and blood. . . . Thackeray and Dickens, having done with earthly houses, live most certainly in our brains" (*Essays* 1:35). The world of the imagination, for writer and for reader, is not simply more beguiling, but more real, more palpable, and more enduring than earthly reality.

Early in 1905, as she began to publish her first reviews and essays, Woolf wrote her contribution to F. W. Maitland's *The Life and Letters of Leslie Stephen*, a daughter's reminiscence of her father. It is a portrait of a man deeply engaged with his children, attentive to their childlike interests, humorous, even playful with them: "My impression as a child always was that my father was not very much older than we were." She recalls his taking them to sail their boats in the Round Pond, and with his own hands fitting out one of the boats with masts and sails. Every evening he spent an hour and a half with the children in the drawing room and found some way of amusing them himself, drawing pictures of animals "as fat as we could demand them" or cutting the shapes of animals out of paper with a pair of scissors.

But the most vivid memories are of her father reading aloud to his children:

> I cannot remember any book before *Tom Brown's School Days* and *Treasure Island;* but it must have been very soon that we attacked the first of that long line of red backs—the thirty-two volumes of the Waverley Novels, which provided reading for many years of evenings, because when we had finished the last he was ready to begin the first over again. At the end of a volume my father always gravely asked our opinion as to its merits, and we were required to say which of the characters we liked best and why. I can remember his indignation when one of us preferred the hero to the far more lifelike villain. My father always loved reading aloud, and of all books, I think, he loved Scott's the best. (*Essays* 1:127–28)

She goes on to write of her father's memory for poetry: if he liked something, it "stuck" to him, he said, and so he acquired a large store of poems which he recited to his children rather than reading from a book: "As he lay back in his chair and spoke the beautiful words with closed eyes, we felt that he was speaking not merely the words of Tennyson or Wordsworth but what he himself felt and knew. Thus many of the great English poems now seem to me inseparable from my father; I hear in them not only his voice, but in some sort his teaching and belief" (129).

Woolf wrote about her father at many points in her life, and the picture is full of contradictions—contradictions that are not resolved over time. The warmth and tenderness of the early portrait, written within a year of his death, contrasts with the fictional portrait of her father as Mr. Ramsay in *To the Lighthouse:* striding into the scene to spoil his son's pleasure, needy and demanding of his wife, endlessly preoccupied with the magnitude of his own achievement. And in a much-quoted entry in her diary, more than twenty years after his death, she wrote, "28 November, 1928. He would have been 96, yes, today; & could have been 96, like other people one has known; but mercifully was not. His life would have entirely ended mine. What would have happened? No writing, no books;—inconceivable" (*Diary* 3:208).

Yet only a year earlier she had written to Vita Sackville-West about *To the Lighthouse:* "I don't know if I'm like Mrs. Ramsay: as my mother died when I was 13 probably it is a child's view of her.... She has haunted me: but then so did that old wretch my father.... I was more like him than her, I think; and therefore more critical: but he was an adorable man, and somehow, tremendous" (*Letters* 3:374). And in another letter, two years later:

> I like to think of myself tapping at my father's study door, saying very loud and clear "Can I have another volume, father? I've finished this one." Then he would be very pleased and say, "Gracious child, how you gobble!" ... and get up and take down, it may have been the 6th or 7th volume of Gibbons complete works, or Speddings Bacon, or Cowper's Letters. "But my dear, if its worth reading, its worth reading twice" he would say. I have a great devotion for him—what a disinterested man, how high minded, how tender to me, and fierce and intolerable. (*Letters* 4:27)

The contradictions recall the fictional Cam, in the last section of *To the Lighthouse,* struggling to maintain her pact with her brother of silent opposition to their father and tugged at the same time by her compassion for him and by her—the word is Woolf's—"attraction" to him. She places the fictional Cam, like herself as a girl, at the door to her father's library, asking a question of the old gentlemen there, knowing that she pleases them by her inquiry. It is a topos that runs through Woolf's recollections of her father. In the memoir she began in 1939, she recalls herself at age eighteen, going up to her father's study to get a book. Note the loving physical detail of her memory, reaching back forty years: "I would find him swinging in his rocking chair, pipe in mouth. Slowly he would unwrinkle his forehead and come to ground and realise with a very sweet smile that I stood there. Rising he would go to the shelves, put the book back, and ask me gently, kindly: 'What did you make of it?'" ("A Sketch of the Past," 157–58). Looking back on herself at eighteen, she remembers feeling "proud and stimulated, and full of love for this unworldly, very distinguished and lonely man."

One could multiply the contradictions, reflecting the intensity of her love and her rage. He is gentle and fierce, adorable and intolerable. Woolf's writings about her father over the course of a lifetime, in fiction, essays, memoirs, letters, diaries, reflect the way a life is told and retold and a relationship altered as memory shifts in response to the currents of the present.

The last passage I shall quote is from an essay entitled "Leslie Stephen," written when Woolf was fifty. From this vantage point she looks back on the events we observed in the present tense through the lens of her adolescent diary:

> Even today there may be parents who would doubt
> the wisdom of allowing a girl of fifteen the free run
> of a large and quite unexpurgated library. But my

father allowed it. There were certain facts—very briefly, very shyly he referred to them. Yet "Read what you like," he said, and all his books, "mangy and worthless," as he called them, but certainly they were many and various, were to be had without asking. To read what one liked because one liked it, never to pretend to admire what one did not—that was his only lesson in the art of reading. To write in the fewest possible words, as clearly as possible, exactly what one meant—that was his only lesson in the art of writing. ("Leslie Stephen," in *The Captain's Death Bed and Other Essays*, 74–75)

The portraits of Leslie Stephen that his daughter has left are various and contradictory: from the playful father sharing his children's pleasures—indeed nearly their peer—to the morose, self-pitying, self-indulgent man casting his gloom over an entire family, separated from his children by not one but two generations. Through the variegated coloring of these pictures, however, what is most constant is Woolf's profound bond with her father, which she preserved throughout her life through the art of reading and that of writing.

6

"I write of things as I see them"

AGE TWENTY-FOUR TO TWENTY-FIVE

By the spring of 1906, Virginia Woolf, now twenty-four years old, was working regularly as a book reviewer and essayist and continuing to practice her art as a writer of fiction. In a letter to her cousin Madge Vaughan that seems to resume a conversation about her work, she declares, "I write of things as I see them; and I am quite conscious all the time that it is a very narrow, and rather bloodless point of view. . . . But my present feeling is that this vague and dream like world, without love, or heart, or passion, or sex, is the world I really care about, and find interesting. For, though they are dreams to you, and I cant express them at all adequately, these things are perfectly real to me" (*Letters* 1:226–27). In response to criticism, the young writer expresses confidence in her own vision, however partial it may appear.

Letters from this period radiate a sense of well-being. In June, Woolf wrote a two-column piece for the *Times Literary Supplement* on "Wordsworth and the Lakes," for which she received £9.7s — "the largest sum I have ever made at one blow," she announced to Violet Dickinson. In August, Virginia, Vanessa, Thoby, and Adrian rented Blo' Norton Hall, a moated Elizabethan manor house on the Norfolk-Suffolk border between Thetford and Diss. A letter to Violet from the beginning of August shows Virginia in high spirits: "Nessa paints windmills in the afternoon, and I tramp the country for miles with a map, leap ditches, scale walls and desecrate churches, making out beautiful brilliant stories every step of the way. One is actually being — as we geniuses say—transferred to paper at this moment" (*Letters* 1:234).

At Blo' Norton Virginia kept a journal that she used, as she had earlier summer journals, as a sort of sketchbook. Like her letters, it shows her in a relaxed, humorous frame of mind:

> The advantages of a bicycle, almost I would say the advantage, is that it gets you to places. Our grandparents never saw Thetford or Diss, unless it was upon the wedding tour, in a high gig; or upon the Christening of the first born, or some other solemn feast, demanding the sanction of the market town.
>
> But I can ride there in an afternoon; to buy postcards or grapes, or merely to look at certain curious old houses.
>
> A very hot August day, a bare road across a moor, fields of corn & stubble—a haze of wood fire smoke —innumerable pheasants & partridges—white stones—thatched cottages—sign posts—tiny villages—great waggons heaped with corn—sagacious dogs, farmers carts. Compose these all somehow into a picture; I am too lazy to do it. (*A Passionate Apprentice*, 315)

Thoby and Adrian stayed with their sisters for two days, then returned to London. On August 10 they left for Trieste, riding on horseback through Albania to Greece, where they were to be met, in September, by Virginia, Vanessa, and Violet. As the month at Blo' Norton went on, Virginia was "chafing" to be off. "Think of Athens and Olympia and Delphi!!!" she wrote excitedly to Violet.

On September 8, Thoby's twenty-sixth birthday, the three women left England, traveled through France and Italy, and sailed for Patras, joining Thoby and Adrian on September 13 at Olympia. Together they visited Corinth, Athens, Nauplia, and Mycenae. On their return journey to Athens, Vanessa fell ill. She recovered sufficiently to continue to Constantinople, but there she again fell ill, and Virginia, Adrian, and Violet brought her back to London on the Orient Express.

When they arrived in London on November 1, they found that Thoby, who had returned ahead, was in bed with a fever. At first he was thought to have malaria or pneumonia; after ten days he was diagnosed with typhoid. During Thoby's illness, Virginia's letters to Violet Dickinson become again, as they were during the illness of her father, both tender and childlike. She turns to Violet with yearnings to be held and comforted, the yearnings of a small girl toward her mother. The old, familiar nicknames return: "I feel myself curled up snugly in old mother wallabies pouch. My little claws nestle round my furry cheeks. Is mother wallaby soft and tender to her little one? He will come and lick her poor lean mangy face. . . . When you wake in the night, I suppose you feel my arms round you" (November 14).

As in the period of her father's illness, her longing for maternal comfort is suffused with erotic feeling, the touch of the mother becoming that of the lover: "Shall we say Love? If you could put your hand in that nest of fur where my heart beats you would feel the thump of the steadiest organ in London—all beating for my Violet. Sometimes when I am ordering dinner, or emptying—a flower vase—a great tide runs from my toe to my crown, which is the thought of you. . . . Now then will you believe that I am devoted to every hair, and every ridge and every hollow, and every spot upon your body. . . . Wallaby wipes his tender nose, and nuzzles you" (*Letters* 1:245). It was an old, fond habit to refer to Violet as a kangeroo and to herself as her baby: Virginia, who often gave affectionate animal nicknames to those she loved, chose as her emblem of Violet an animal who carries her young within her very body. Five days after Virginia wrote this poignant letter, on November 20, 1906, Thoby died.

At first, Virginia's letters to Violet make no mention of Thoby's death: Violet herself was extremely ill after their return from Greece, and it was thought necessary that she be protected for as long as possible from learning that Thoby had died. Virginia kept up the pretense until December 18, when Violet, reading a review of Maitland's *Life of Leslie Stephen* which referred to the recent untimely death of his son, learned the truth.

In a letter to Violet written on December 10, while Virginia was still withholding the fact of Thoby's death, she speaks of her affection for her father's biographer, who was also a family friend, and whom she had recently seen just before he left for Teneriffe. He had brought a packet of letters about the book, and two of them, she boasted, had said that her own part was "beautifully done." On the voyage to Teneriffe, however, Maitland developed pneumonia, and on December 19 he too died. "The earth seems swept very bare," Virginia wrote to Violet, "and the amount of pain that accumulates for some one to feel grows every day" (December 23, 1906).

Letters from this period are relatively silent about Thoby, but Woolf would write about him years later in her memoir. It was Thoby who had introduced her to the ancient Greeks; it was he who first told her the story of Hector and Troy. When he was home from school on holidays, they argued about Shakespeare, walking up and down the stairs, "too shy with each other to be still." Thoby told her stories about the boys at his school, first Evelyns, then Clifton: "I knew all his friends through those stories." And when Thoby went up to Cambridge, the friends he made there became her friends too; one of them would become her husband. Through Thoby's stories of life at school and through her acquaintance with his Cambridge circle, Virginia saw a brother's education that was altogether unlike her own. At twenty-one she wrote to him at Cambridge, "I dont get anybody to argue with me now, and feel the want. I have to delve from books, painfully and all alone, what you get every evening sitting over your fire and smoking your pipe with Strachey etc. No wonder my knowledge is scant. Theres nothing like talk as an educator I'm sure" (*Letters* 1:77).

In her memoir she describes a scene with Thoby, one of her earliest memories, she says. It is of herself and Thoby on the lawn pummeling each other: "Just as I raised my fist to hit him, I felt: why hurt another person? I dropped my hand instantly, and stood there, and let him beat me. I remember the feeling. It was a feeling of hopeless sadness. It was as if I became aware of something terrible; and of my own powerlessness. I slunk off alone, feeling horribly depressed." To call this one of her earliest memories underscores its importance to her: the picture of herself giving up the fight with her brother and ending by feeling "powerless," "alone," and "horribly depressed" is a metaphor that distills into a single scene deep currents of feeling and fantasy. The image surfaces in a work of fiction.

Critics have considered the novel *Jacob's Room* to be Woolf's elegy for her brother. Certainly the biographical parallels invite this view: a young man thought to be full of promise who dies at twenty-six, the Cambridge education, the close friendships formed there, the trip to Greece—the bare facts of Jacob's story are clearly drawn from Thoby's life.

When she tried to imagine what Thoby might have become in later years had he lived, she stopped, arrested by the phrase "had he lived." She reflected that the knell of those words affected her memory of a time when in fact they were not heard at all. It was impossible to recapture her relationship with her brother as it had actually felt when they were young. They had no foreboding that he was to die; she did not see him then, as she did now, with all his promise ended. Thinking back to their animated conversations when he was home from school on vacation, she found that the knell of his later death inevitably sounded through those earlier conversations so that it became impossible, finally, to remember Thoby as he was, or the excitement of those discussions, innocent of the knowledge that they would end, suddenly, when he was twenty-six and she twenty-four.

About Jacob Flanders, too, we hear that knell, always. It is not until the last page of the novel that the reader is told of his death, but it is prefigured from the first. Woolf's first readers in 1922, as Zwerdling (1986) points out, would instantly have associated the name Flanders with death in battle: nearly a third of British soldiers killed in the Great War lost their lives there.

> In Flanders fields, the poppies blow
> Between the crosses, row on row . . .
> We are the Dead. Short days ago
> We lived, felt dawn, saw sunset glow,
>   Loved and were loved, and now we lie
>   In Flanders fields.

Jacob's mother, Betty Flanders, is a widow with three young sons. We are told that she had had carved on her husband's tombstone "Merchant of this city," although he had only sat behind an office window for three months and before that had run a little wild. This passing detail is a pointed one: the way the living falsify the dead in retrospect mattered greatly to Virginia Woolf. Reaching to take hold of her mother in memory, she was vexed by the way Julia Stephen was idealized in the accounts that others gave of her, robbed of particularity. *Jacob's Room* is a novel that refuses to idealize the dead.

To the extent that *Jacob's Room* draws upon Woolf's feelings about her brother Thoby, it is a highly ambivalent portrait. For all the novel's mournfulness, there is also bitterness and envy. Jacob Flanders himself, whom we follow from boyhood to young manhood, remains, in the end, a cipher. Critics have seen this novel, Woolf's first experimental fiction, the beginning of her modernist enterprise, as showing the unknowableness of personality. After a succession of broken-off, partial comments about Jacob—by Clara Durrant, Julia Eliot, Mr. Sopwith, Betty Flanders, Captain Barfoot—the narrator states, "Life is but a procession of shadows, and God knows why it is that we embrace them so eagerly, and see them depart with such anguish, being shadows. . . . A young man appears of all things in the world the most real, the most solid, the best known to us" but "the moment after we know nothing about him."

It is true that we know little about Jacob, even by the end of the novel, but is this because personality is unknowable or because there is little to know about him? The other characters idealize him extravagantly: At the dance on Guy Fawkes night, as Jacob stands against the wall smoking a pipe, two of the dancers break off from the rest, bow before him, and tell him that he is the most beautiful man they have ever seen. They wreathe his head with paper flowers, he is made to sit on a white and gilt chair, and glass grapes are hung on his shoulders. Jacob's passivity in this scene is characteristic: we see him through the eyes of various women—Florinda, Fanny Elmer, Clara Durrant, Sandra Wentworth Williams—but he himself remains largely silent and disengaged. Dick Graves tells Helen Askew that he thought Jacob the greatest man he had ever known. Helen replies that she thought them both heroes, and the friendship between them so much more beautiful than women's friendships.

It is in friendships with men, especially at Cambridge, that the picture of Jacob comes most vividly to life, and here it is impossible to escape the comparison with Thoby. Like Thoby,

Jacob has a circle of friends at Cambridge who have a large sense of their own importance: "The flesh and blood of the future depends entirely upon six young men. And as Jacob was one of them, no doubt he looked a little regal and pompous as he turned his page, and Julia Hedge disliked him naturally enough" (*Jacob's Room*, 107). Who is Julia Hedge? She appears very briefly, described as "a feminist" who, in the British Museum, reads the names of great men inscribed all round the dome and asks, "Why didn't they leave room for an Eliot or a Brontë?" A minor figure here, Julia Hedge anticipates the first-person narrator of *A Room of One's Own*, doing research at the British Museum on the question of why women have so small a place in the history of literature. Julia's angry question, as she looks up at the splendid dome of the British Museum inscribed with the names of men only, is Woolf's own.

In Jacob's friendships at Cambridge there is a sort of mutual narcissism that allows the young men to feel larger than life. The self-importance of Jacob and Timothy Durrant is mocked in the narrative: "They were boastful, triumphant; it seemed to both that they had read every book in the world; known every sin, passion, and joy. Civilizations stood round them like flowers ready for the picking. Ages lapped at their feet like waves fit for sailing" (76). Opinions are the currency of their friendships, and the men are given to making foolishly grandiose pronouncements: "It was only the French who could paint. . . . Why read anything but Marlowe and Shakespeare, Jacob said, and Fielding if you must read novels?" (122).

One of the few times readers are made privy to Jacob's thoughts is in a scene in King's College Chapel. He thinks that allowing women to take part in the service would be like bringing a dog into church, which might wander down the aisle, lift a paw, and approach a pillar "with a purpose that makes the blood run cold with horror."

Thus Woolf gives to Jacob, as a Cambridge undergraduate, an unthinking contempt for women and a conviction that women rightly are excluded from the world that is his by birthright. Cambridge is "like a suburb where you go to see a view and eat a special cake! 'We are the sole purveyors of this cake.'" In the Cambridge night, the stroke of the clock is muffled, "as if generations of learned men heard the last hour go rolling through their ranks and issued it, already smooth and time-worn, with their blessing, for the use of the living." The past itself is the gift of these learned men to the living, and, smoking his pipe, Jacob "looked satisfied; indeed masterly . . . himself the inheritor" (45).

However banal Jacob is shown to be, however little he really cares that his volume of Shakespeare is knocked overboard, however silly and self-congratulatory the conversations of Cambridge undergraduates are, this is Jacob's world. He is indeed the inheritor.

In a scene in their Cambridge rooms, Jacob listens to his friend Simeon speaking, Jacob himself saying only "hum" or nothing at all. We do not hear his words, if indeed he speaks. But we do hear the sharp tap of a pipe on the mantelpiece, the sound signaling that this is a man's world. The tap of the pipe and the mantelpiece itself recall the letter Virginia wrote to her brother when he was at Cambridge: "I have to delve from books, painfully and all alone, what you get every evening sitting over your fire and smoking your pipe with Strachey etc. No wonder my knowledge is scant."

Like her brother, Jacob journeys to Greece after Cambridge. There he preens his perceptions to be displayed on his return: "'You ought to have been in Athens,' he would say to his friend Bonamy when he got back. 'Standing on the Parthenon,' he would say, or 'The ruins of the Coliseum suggest some fairly sublime reflections,' which he would write out at length in letters." But as readers, we never hear those reflections or see those letters. We see only the magnitude of his ambition. Jacob's interior monologue continues: "It might turn to an essay upon civilization. A comparison between the ancients and moderns, with some pretty sharp hits at Mr. Asquith—something in the style of Gibbon" (136). Jacob writes to Bonamy that he intends to come to Greece every year so long as he lives, that it is "the only chance I can see of protecting oneself from civilization" (146). Bonamy cannot imagine what Jacob could mean by that, yet he feels somehow impressed.

To the extent that *Jacob's Room* draws upon Woolf's feelings about her brother Thoby, it is a satiric portrait. The young man is fully at home in the Cambridge world from which Virginia Woolf, as a woman, was excluded. She would dramatize this exclusion in *A Room of One's Own*. In Oxbridge the narrator, preparing her lecture "Women and Fiction," is walking across the grass of one of the colleges absorbed in thought. She finds her thought interrupted by a man gesticulating at her, his face expressing horror and indignation. "He was a Beadle; I was a woman. This was the turf; there was the path. Only the Fellows and Scholars are allowed here; the gravel is the place for me." And again when she wants to look at a manuscript in the library, a "gentleman" tells her that "ladies are only admitted to the library if accompanied by a Fellow of the College or furnished with a letter of introduction." The narrator's response to being turned aside reflects on the character of Jacob Flanders and his Cambridge circle: "I thought how unpleasant it is to be locked out; and I thought how it is worse perhaps to be locked in" (24).

In a memorable passage in *A Room of One's Own*, the narrator speculates on what would have been her fate had Shakespeare had a sister. The girl was as gifted as her brother, "as adventurous, as imaginative, as agog to see the world as he was. But she was not sent to school. She had no chance of learning grammar and logic, let alone of reading Horace and Virgil. She picked up a book now and then, one of her brother's perhaps, and read a few pages. But then her parents came in and told her to mend the stockings or mind the stew and not moon about with books and papers" (*A Room of One's Own*, 49). Judith Shakespeare would have been denied a formal education and, even more important, denied that varied experience of life that educated her brother: "She could get no training in her craft. Could she even seek her dinner in a tavern or roam the streets at midnight? Yet her genius was for fiction and lusted to feed abundantly upon the lives of men and women and the study of their ways." In the end, thwarted by circumstance and tormented by the contradictions of her own feelings, Shakespeare's sister kills herself: "Who shall measure the heat and violence of the poet's heart when caught and mangled in a woman's body."

Woolf was herself a sister, and she was acutely aware of having been denied all that was given to her brothers. If *Jacob's Room* is an elegy for Thoby, it is a bitter, envious, ambivalent elegy. What is most sympathetic about its central character is the senselessness of his death.[1]

Thoby's death was quickly followed by a loss of another sort for Virginia: two days later, Vanessa agreed to marry Thoby's Cambridge friend Clive Bell. Virginia's letters, nearly silent about the death of Thoby, repeatedly express sorrow and anger at the

1. Similarly Percival in *The Waves*, who has also been thought by critics to be drawn from Thoby, dies senselessly at twenty-five, thrown from a horse. Percival is given a name that suggests mythological grandeur, but little human particularity. He is silent, and is seen through the extravagant idealization of the other characters, to whom he is a hero likened to Ajax and Hector. As Caws (1991) points out, he has been transformed into a myth, the noble knight-on-horseback, Percival.

intrusion of Clive Bell into her relationship with her sister: "It does seem strange and intolerable sometimes. When I think of father and Thoby and then see that funny little creature twitching his pink skin and jerking out his little spasm of laughter I wonder what odd freak there is in Nessa's eyesight. But I dont say this, and wont say it, except to you." This letter to Violet ends, "I run to a book as a child to its mother" (December 30, 1906). Virginia tried to find consolation in the way she always had. And she tried, by an effort of will, to reconcile herself to this new loss: "I did not see Nessa alone, but I realize that that is all over, and I shall never see her alone any more; and Clive is a new part of her, which I must learn to accept" (January 3, 1907).

Vanessa and Clive were married on February 7, 1907. In letters to her new brother-in-law, an erotic aura surrounds her tenderness to her sister: "Give my love to my sister, and, if you like, kiss her left eye, with the eyelid smoothed over the curve, and just blue on the crest" (March 22, 1907); "Both eyes are to be kissed, the tip of the right ear, and the snout if its wet" (August 18, 1907). But letters to Violet have a tone of bitterness that only intensified when Vanessa became pregnant: "Nessa comes tomorrow—what one calls Nessa; but it means husband and baby, and of sister there is less than there used to be." Surprisingly, this letter is dated August 25, 1907—five months before the baby was due. Virginia goes on to speak of her writing projects: the associative link between Vanessa's baby and her writing appears often in letters at this time. Writing to Violet the next week, she complains, "To be with her is to sit in autumn sunlight; but then there is Clive! Now I must set myself down to my novel (review), and then to my 7 poetic dramas; shall I ever bear a child I wonder?" (*Letters* 1:309). And a few weeks later, while on holiday with Vanessa and Clive: "I see how I shall spend my days a virgin, an Aunt, an authoress." She feels an outsider to their self-sufficient contentment: "My God, they are a happy couple! I used to think it might be intermittent, but now I see with pulse serene the very heart of the machine—how for weeks together they seem to hover over the same flower. We have gone on, having picnics and walks and so forth, you will tell me how fortunate and happy I am. We go back on Thursday, and I want to write for six months unceasingly" (*Letters* 1:311). The next month she wrote to Vanessa, "But why should I intrude upon your circle of bliss? Especially when I can think of nothing but my novel." This is one of the first references to the work that would be published ultimately as *The Voyage Out*.

During the summer of 1907, when Virginia joined Vanessa and Clive on holiday, she speaks of her sister's pregnancy as though there already were a baby, further crowding her away from Vanessa. It was at this time she began work on her gift for the baby-to-be: a "life" of Vanessa. But, as Schulkind (1985) points out, "No meaningful distinction can be made here between biography [of Vanessa] and autobiography." What Virginia Woolf wrote, at twenty-five, was a memoir. In addressing it to the next generation, she was continuing a family tradition: her grandfather James Stephen had written his memoirs for his children, and her father, too, after the death of his wife, had written a memoir that he addressed to his children and stepchildren. Sir Leslie's memoir was a response to loss, as was Virginia's.

At this time Virginia wrote lives of Violet Dickinson and of her aunts Caroline Emilia Stephen and Mary Fisher. The lives of her aunts do not survive, but the "Life" of Violet, also written in 1907, is an exuberant, whimsical flight of the imagination. Her "Life" of Vanessa is altogether different in tone. Ostensibly addressed to the new baby, it was written to recapture what Virginia herself had lost. As she said in a letter to Clive, "I have been writing Nessa's life; and I am going to send you 2 chapters in a day or two. It might have been so good! As it is, I am too near, and too far; and it seems to be blurred, and I ask myself why write it at all? seeing I never shall recapture what you have, by your side this minute" (April 15, 1908).

Addressed to the expected baby, the "Life" of Vanessa begins, "Your mother was born in 1879" but soon broadens its focus to become a history of the Stephen family to the time when Vanessa was eighteen and Virginia fifteen. The narrative is organized around two deaths, first that of Julia Stephen and then that of Stella. But death enters the story even before it begins: Julia's first marriage is very much a part of the narrative—the marriage that ended in the sudden death of her husband, leaving Julia Duckworth a widow with young children at twenty-four: "When he was dead she determined to consecrate those years as the golden ones; when as she phrased it perhaps, she had not known the sorrow and the crime of the world because she had lived with a man, stainless of his kind, exalted in a world of love and beauty."

There clung to Julia what her daughter called "an enduring melancholy." When she came to know Leslie Stephen, it was only reluctantly that she could turn from her "habit of suffering," could accept that "joy was to be endured as well as sorrow." Perhaps Julia's "enduring melancholy" accounts, in part, for the difficulty her daughter would have in remembering her. There is a bitter edge to the picture of Julia as otherwise engaged, looking backward to a golden age, as if her real life were there, not here: "It is notable that she never spoke of her first love; and in treasuring it changed it perhaps to something far fairer than it could have been, had life allowed it to endure." Woolf recognized the advantage that the dead have over the living: they can be idealized without the contradiction that day-to-day experience provides.

She observes that it is difficult to describe those who have died in a way that retains their human vitality. "Written words," she observes, "tend most unfortunately to drape themselves in smooth folds annulling all evidence of life. . . . It has often occurred to me to regret that no one ever wrote down her sayings and vivid ways of speech" ("Reminiscences," 36).

In the memoir that Woolf wrote many years later, the picture of her mother is more sharply etched. The early one lacks the vividness of anecdote, of incident. It seems at times a representation sculpted in marble, beautiful but cool to the touch: "Her most trivial activities had something of grandeur about them; and her presence was large and austere, bringing with it not only joy and life, exquisite fleeting femininities, but the majesty of a nobly composed human being." This is not a person whom we recognize as having human particularity, nor is the author's voice one we recognize. It is self-conscious and strained. In Woolf's essays and book reviews, even at this early period, the voice is more distinctly her own. Here her own voice is muted by all that she was struggling not to say.

In writing about her father, however, she gives free rein to her rage. It is three years since she wrote lovingly about him in her contribution to Maitland's biography and in her letters over the long period of his dying. Here she gives a dark and angry picture of a man colossal in his neediness after the death of Julia: "All those tears and groans, reproaches and protestations of affection, high talk of duty and work and living for others, were doubtless what we should feel if we felt properly, and yet we had but a dull sense of gloom which could not honestly be referred to the dead; unfortunately it did not quicken our feeling for the living; but hideous as it was, obscured both living and dead; and for long did unpardonable mischief by substituting for the shape of a true and most vivid mother, nothing better than an unlovable phantom" ("Reminiscence," 45). Coercive and melodramatic, he made it impossible for the children to grieve for the death of their mother: and the picture of Julia that emerges in the pages of this memoir is indeed that of "an unlovable phantom."

Yet for all the fury of this portrayal, Virginia steps back, at one point, to reflect: "We made him the type of all that we hated in our lives. . . . We were bitter, harsh, and to a great extent, unjust; but even now it seems to me that there was some truth in our complaint; and sufficient reason why both parties should be unable at the time and without fault, to come to a good understanding. If he had been ten years younger, or we older, or had there been a mother or sister to intervene, much pain and anger and loneliness might have been spared" ("Reminiscence," 56). Even in the fullness of her rage, she poses the question of whether the story she was telling was the whole story.

Woolf would revisit this time again in her later memoir, taking up from another vantage point the people and events she had described at twenty-five. She began it on April 18, 1939, at the age of fifty-eight, and the last entry is dated November 17, 1940, four months before her death.

Memory itself is an important subject of this memoir. One of the problems, she declares at the outset, is "the enormous number of things I can remember," and she decides simply to push straight through: "So without stopping to choose my way . . . I begin: the first memory. This was of red and purple flowers on a black ground—my mother's dress; and she was sitting either in a train or in an omnibus, and I was on her lap." And then she adds another memory: in dreamlike fashion, she is not troubled that this seems also to be her first memory. "It is of lying half asleep, half awake, in bed in the nursery in St. Ives" and hearing the waves breaking and "hearing the blind draw its little acorn across the floor as the wind blew the blind out." She goes on to make some observations about the nature of childhood impressions—how inseparable are the senses from one another, so that "pictures" is not quite the right word for these memories. And then she adds what she calls a "digression":

> Those moments—in the nursery, on the road to the beach—can still be more real than the present moment. . . . I can reach a state where I seem to be watching things happen as if I were there. That is, I suppose, that my memory supplies what I had forgotten, so that it seems as if it were happening independently, though I am really making it happen. In certain favourable moods, memories—what one has forgotten—come to the top. Now if this is so, is it not possible—I often wonder—that things we have felt with great intensity have an existence independent of our minds; are in fact still in existence? And if so, will it not be possible, in time, that some device will be invented by which we can tap them? I see it—the past—as an avenue lying behind; a long ribbon of scenes, emotions. There at the end of the avenue still, are the garden and the nursery. Instead of remembering here a scene, there a sound, I shall fit a plug into the wall; and listen in to the past. I shall turn up August 1890. I feel that strong emotion must leave its trace; and it is only a question of discovering how we can get ourself again attached to it, so we shall be able to live our lives through from the start. ("A Sketch of the Past," 67)

Far more has been preserved than is readily available to conscious recollection. At different times, in different states, memories may become more accessible or more vivid, and Woolf imagines an electrical device by which memories that are seemingly lost can be recovered. But she carries the notion further, to imagine that not only could memories be recovered, but the past itself. It is a beguiling fancy, and a poignant one.

Interestingly, she singles out as an example of a memory that cannot change the memory of three individuals who died when she was a child: "I see them exactly as I saw them." Unaltered by subsequent experience, the dead are fixed forever in her memory. Or so she asserts here.

But when she comes to write about her mother, she must acknowledge that in fact the past is not so retrievable as she had wished, and death itself does not make memories any less mutable: "If it were true, as I said above, that the things that ceased in childhood are easy to describe because they are complete, then it should be easy to say what I felt for my mother, who died when I was 13. Thus I should be able to see her completely undisturbed by later impressions, as I saw Mr. Gibbs & C. B. Clarke. But the theory, though true of them, breaks down completely with her" ("A Sketch of the Past," 80).

She recalls of her mother,

> I see her in her white dressing gown on the balcony; and the passion flower with the purple star on its petals. Her voice is still faintly in my ears—decided, quick; and in particular the little drops with which her laughter ended—three diminishing ahs ... "Ah—ah—ah." I sometimes end a laugh that way myself. And I see her hands, like Adrian's, with the very individual square-tipped fingers, each finger with a waist to it, and the nail broadening out. (My own are the same size all the way, so that I can slip a ring over my thumb.) She had three rings; a diamond ring, an emerald ring, and an opal ring. My eyes used to fix themselves upon the lights in the

opal as it moved across the page of the lesson book when she taught us, and I was glad that she left it to me. . . . Also I hear the tinkle of her bracelets, made of twisted silver, given her by Mr Lowell, as she went about the house; especially as she came up at night to see if we were asleep, holding a candle shaded; this is a distinct memory, for like all children, I lay awake sometimes and longed for her to come. ("A Sketch of the Past," 81–82)

Having brought to the surface these fragments of memory, she asks, "But can I get any closer to her without drawing upon all those descriptions and anecdotes which after she was dead imposed themselves upon my view of her?" Memory itself must be the medium through which she approaches her mother, and the effort fails: "If I turn to my mother how difficult it is to single her out as she really was; to imagine what she was thinking, to put a single sentence into her mouth! I dream; I make up pictures of a summer's afternoon" (87).

   She finds that she cannot recapture what she did not have: "When I think of her spontaneously she is always in a room full of people. . . . What a jumble of things I can remember, if I let my mind run, about my mother; but they are all of her in company; of her surrounded; of her generalised; dispersed" (84). Woolf tries from her present vantage point as an adult to explain or understand her mother's unavailability. She tries to look at her mother not as a child, but as a woman who is herself now older than her mother was when she died: "The understanding that I now have of her position must have its say; and it shows me that a woman of forty with seven children, some of them needing grown up attention, and four still in the nursery; and an eighth, Laura, an idiot, yet living with us; and a husband fifteen years her elder, difficult, exacting, dependent on her; I see now that woman who had to keep all this in being and under control must have been a general presence rather than a particular person to a child of seven or eight" ("A Sketch of the Past," 83). But all the reasonableness she marshals seems to crumble when she returns to her experience as a child: "Can I remember ever being alone with her for more than a few minutes? Someone was always interrupting."

Though Woolf's fancy was that memory waits, a ribbon that can be reeled in at will, what she found, in fact, was that her memories of her mother were meager and insufficient, and moreover subject to revision. She was vexed to find that with the passage of time, her memory of her mother had become "rubbed out and featureless," "dominated by the beauty of her face—and inevitably" ("A Sketch of the Past," 85).

What Woolf writes about her mother's own early life is punctuated by uncertainty and questions: "She was born, I think, in 1848 [actually 1846]; I think in India. . . . An old governess—was she Mable Rose? did she give her the picture of Beatrice that hung in the dining room at Talland House?" Her mother had spent much of her girlhood and young womanhood at Little Holland House, the home of her aunt and uncle, a gathering place for writers and artists:

> Little Holland House was her world then. But what was that world like? I think of it as a summer afternoon world. To my thinking Little Holland House is an old white country house, standing in a large garden. Long windows open onto the lawn. Through them comes a stream of ladies in crinolines and little straw hats; they are attended by gentlemen in pet-top trousers and whiskers. The date is round about 1860. It is a hot summer day. Tea tables with great bowls of strawberries and cream are scat-

tered about the lawn. They are 'presided over' by some of the six lovely sisters; who do not wear crinolines, but are robed in splendid Venetian draperies; they sit enthroned . . . My mother comes out of the window wearing that striped silk dress buttoned at the throat with a glowing skirt that appears in the photograph. She is of course 'a vision' as they used to say; and there she stands, silent, with her plate of strawberries and cream. ("A Sketch of the Past," 86–87)

Having had to ask herself what Little Holland House was like, Woolf conjures it into being, her fictional imagination filling in what a mother's report could not.

In writing about her mother, Woolf is straining after facts and aware that much of what she writes is necessarily conjectural. Any bit of history, any family anecdote is turned over and over in her hands, a scrap of evidence from which to draw inferences. She knew that once her mother went to a river party wearing a hat with great feathers and that her Aunt Caroline was surprised to see her standing alone rather than at the center of a bevy of admirers. "Where are they?" she asked Anny Thackeray and was told, "Oh, they don't happen to be here today." Woolf draws from this brief exchange "a little scene which makes me suspect that Julia aged seventeen or eighteen was aloof; and shed a certain silence around her by her very beauty. That little scene is dated; she cannot have been more than eighteen; because she married when she was nineteen" (88–89).

After the death of her first husband, Julia told a friend, "I have been as unhappy and as happy as it is possible for a human being to be." Woolf repeats the formula several times, in a tone of controlled bitterness: "What my mother was like when she was as happy as anyone can be, I have no notion. Not a sound or a scene has survived from those four years" (89). What she does know is that after the death of her husband, Julia Duckworth lost her faith. And this, too, Woolf examines as a clue to the character of her mother: "It proves that there was more in her than simplicity. . . . There was complexity in her. . . . Probably it was that combination that accounted for the great impression she made on people . . . The certain fact at any rate is that when she was left alone . . . she began to think out her position; and for this reason perhaps read something my father had written" ("A Sketch of the Past," 90). "It proves," "probably," "perhaps": Woolf makes use of what facts she has and must infer the rest. Of her mother's early life she knows little: she must summon Little Holland House into being through the vividness of her imagination. Of her mother's character, too, she knows less than she would wish: from the evidence she has, she makes deductions, draws conclusions. Perhaps the necessity—the urgent necessity—to flesh out the bare bones that memory can supply helps to develop the fictional imagination. It is not just that early loss leaves the individual with memories that are too few, too meager, and unsustaining. Memories of the dead, Woolf found, are mutable. She could not simply reel in the ribbon, as she had wished.

The difficulty she encountered in trying to recapture her mother was reflected on a wider scale. As her mother had proved elusive to the reach of memory, so women elude the reach of historical memory. It is a theme she explored to brilliant effect in *A Room of One's Own*. And as she used her fictional imagination to fill in what she could not know about the earlier life of her own mother—Woolf herself setting strawberries and cream on the table at Little Holland House—she tried to flesh out what little is known about the few women writers before the eighteenth century. Information is meager indeed: "When one comes to seek out facts about Lady Winchelsea, one finds, as usual, that almost nothing is known about her." She was a poet; she was born in 1661; she "suffered terribly from melancholy" (*A Room of One's Own,* 63). Repeatedly in her attempt to find out more about the lives of women, the first-person narrator comes up against an absence: "What I find deplorable, I continued, looking about the bookshelves again, is that nothing is known about women before the eighteenth century. I have no model in my mind to turn about this way and that" (47). Searching, she discovers only "blank spaces on the shelves." She finds that she is "looking about on shelves for books that were not there."

To search after something that is not there was an experience Woolf knew well. We think back through our mothers if we are women—but how to think back through them if we know almost nothing about them? Trying to imagine what the life of an Elizabethan woman would have been, she finds that "one is held up by the scarcity of facts. One knows nothing detailed, nothing perfectly true and substantial about her" (46). Woolf is speaking about the loss of women to the record of history, but she could equally be speaking about her mother, absent from her personal history: "She never writes her own life and scarcely keeps a diary; there are only a handful of her letters in existence. She left no plays or poems by which we can judge her. What one wants . . . is a mass of information" (47).

Woolf points out that although women are absent from the record of history, their own voices silent, they are preeminent in the imaginations of others. In the British Museum the narrator of *A Room of One's Own* finds an avalanche of books about women—women as they live in the minds of men: "Imaginatively she is of the highest importance; practically she is completely insignificant. She pervades poetry from cover to cover; she is all but absent from history . . . Some of the more inspired words, some of the most profound thoughts in literature fall from her lips; in real life she could hardly read, could scarcely spell, and was the property of her husband (45–46). She draws a stark contrast between woman's place in "real life" and her place in the imaginative lives of others, a distinction with deep personal resonance. Those we have lost are not absent; indeed they are all the more present for being so readily available to imagination and fantasy.

Woolf was interested not only in the relative absence of women writers before the rise of the novel, she was interested in the absence of women from history, the absence, that is, of the ordinary, the vast majority of women as well as of the extraordinary and the gifted. History gives no record of their lives. "At what age did she marry; how many children had she as a rule; what was her house like; had she a room to herself; did she do the cooking; would she be likely to have a servant?" (47). Here Woolf's imagination creates a scene of mother and daughter, an elderly woman crossing the street on the arm of her middle-aged daughter: if one were to ask the elder woman about her life, she might well say she could remember nothing: "For all the dinners are cooked; the plates and cups washed; the children set to school and gone out into the world. Nothing remains of it all. All has vanished. No biography or history has a word to say about it. And the novels, without meaning to, inevitably lie. All these infinitely obscure lives remain to be recorded" (93).

The recording of "these infinitely obscure lives" interested Woolf as early as age twenty-four. On holiday at Blo' Norton in August 1906, she wrote a short piece of fiction entitled "The Journal of Mistress Joan Martyn." In form, it is a story within a story: both the framing story and the story enclosed within it have as their theme the loss of women to historical memory. The female narrator, who introduces herself as Miss Rosamond Merridew, describes herself as a historian of medieval England whose research concerns the system of land tenure in the thirteenth, fourteenth, and fifteenth centuries. She goes on to tell of having found, among the family papers of a farmer, a manuscript that was the diary of his "grandmother Joan," written when the author was twenty-five years old.

Thus Woolf imagines into being the diary of a woman close to her own age, born in 1495.[2] The beginning of the story-within-the-story, the "Journal" of Mistress Joan Martyn, describes the coming of evening and her mother's closing of the "Gates" (capitalized throughout) of the estate. The home she loves is a matriarchy, a female world in which men are present only peripherally. Her father is off in London and her brothers are in the army; it is her mother who presides: "It is a great thing to be the daughter of such a woman, and to hope that one day the same power may be mine. She rules us all." The gates of the estate are kept locked in order to protect those within from danger, inevitably associated with men: "I am glad to draw close to the fire, and to think that all those bad men who prowl in the lanes, and lie hidden in the woods at this hour cannot break through our great Gates, try as they will." The rattle of the door, she fears, is the battering ram of a highwayman; as gusts of wind lift the tapestry in her room, she imagines the figures in the cloth to be men in armor charging down upon her.

Mistress Joan Martyn is reluctant to marry. She does so only because it is the condition necessary for a woman to have a place in the social order: "No other event in the life of a woman can mean so great a change; for from flitting shadow-like and unconsidered in her father's house, marriage suddenly forms her to a substantial body, with weight which people must see and

2. The year is an oversight: a woman born in the late fifteenth century would of course be further removed than a grandmother to the farmer.

make way for." Were it not for this change, however, a change that occurs in the eyes of other people, Joan would prefer to remain as she is, enclosed in the domain of her mother. Marriage, she fears, "would confuse the clear vision which is still mine."

And in the framing story, the historian Miss Rosamond Merridew says of her own life that she "exchanged a husband and a family and a house in which I may grow old for certain fragments of yellow parchment." It is impossible, it seemed to Virginia Woolf at twenty-four, for a woman both to marry and to retain her clear vision.

Joan Martyn might have become a writer: her father is proud of her skill and urges her to preserve her writing. But in her own view, "truly, there is nothing in the pale of my days that needs telling." She would be lost to memory were it not for the curiosity and persistence of the historian Rosamond Merridew. She presses the farmer to show her his ancestral home, and he points with his riding crop at one dark canvas after another, portraits of his ancestors. She observes that they were all portraits of men. Wives and daughters were not preserved in paintings. But in the diary of a twenty-five-year-old woman Rosamond Merridew discovers a self-portrait that, as a historian, she rescues from obscurity.

This early work of fiction anticipates a central theme of *A Room of One's Own:* that the "infinitely obscure lives" of women remain to be written. In undertaking to do this, Woolf says, she felt herself to be "a deliverer advancing with lights across the waste of years to the rescue of some stranded ghost."[3]

In "A Sketch of the Past" Virginia Woolf mentions an interesting fact about her mother: she had been a signator of an antisuffrage petition. In the issue of *Nineteenth Century* for June 1889

3. "The Lives of the Obscure" in *The Common Reader.*

there appeared "An Appeal Against Female Suffrage," signed by Mrs. Leslie Stephen and about one hundred other women. "We believe," these women stated, "that the emancipating process has now reached the limits fixed by the physical constitution of women, and by the fundamental difference which must always exist between their main occupations and those of men." To admit women to the ordinary machinery of political life, they asserted, would blunt the special moral qualities of women, endanger their special contribution to the community, and misconstrue women's special mission.

That her mother signed such an appeal must have been, to her daughter, a dismaying fact. But there is another fact about Julia Stephen that her daughter nowhere mentions, and it is an astonishing omission.

In both her memoirs Woolf wrote mournfully about the difficulty she had in remembering her mother. At twenty-five she wrote, "What would one not give to recapture a single phrase even!" ("Reminiscences," 36). And at fifty-eight, "For what reality can remain real of a person who died forty-four years ago at the age of forty-nine, without leaving a book, or a picture, or any piece of work—apart from the three children who now survive and the memory of her that remains in their minds?" ("A Sketch of the Past," 85).

The fact is that Julia Stephen *did* write a book. It is not a long book or a great book, but it is a book, entitled *Notes from Sick Rooms* and published in London by Smith, Elder, & Co. in October 1883. Moreover, letters from Leslie Stephen two years later indicate that he and Julia were negotiating with Routledge to publish in book form her children's stories, illustrated by him, a project that did not come to fruition.

Notes from Sick Rooms is a series of brief essays offering advice based upon Julia's experience in nursing the sick. The essays are carefully observed and gracefully written. There are passages of some wit, and in the pages of this book we do hear her particular voice. Here, for example, is the beginning of a section called "Crumbs":

> Among the number of small evils which haunt illness, the greatest, in the misery which it can cause, though the smallest in size, is crumbs. The origin of most things has been decided on, but the origin of crumbs in bed has never excited sufficient attention among the scientific world, though it is a problem which has tormented many a weary sufferer. I will forbear to give my own explanation, which would be neither scientific nor orthodox, and will merely beg that their evil existence may be recognised and, as far as human nature allows, guarded against. The torment of crumbs should be stamped out of the sick bed as if it were the Colorado beetle in a potato field. Anyone who has been ill will at once take her precautions, feeble though they will prove. (*Notes from Sick Rooms*, 219)

The experience she draws upon is well within the woman's sphere, surely. But while many women engaged in looking after the sick, it was the rare woman who undertook to write about it. There is a tenderness and attentiveness in her attitude to those in her care, and she writes a well-turned sentence. Julia Stephen is not one of the great lost writers of the nineteenth century, but it is curious that the daughter who was herself a writer and who strained at the meagerness of her memories of her mother, who thought herself so eager to hear her mother's voice, should turn away from the one record she did have of the cadences of her mother's speech. She yearned to hear her mother's voice—and yet she also needed to silence her.

The way that death itself alters our memory of those who

have died is, interestingly, the subject of the final paragraph of Julia Stephen's book: "When the requisite washing has been tenderly done, and the fresh white clothes have been put on, the head, bound up by a silk handkerchief, should be laid on a low pillow, not put perfectly flat; the covering, whatever is wished, should be laid over the body, and then the relations, if they have remained away, return, not indeed to find all that they loved, but not to be shocked by a terrible picture which will haunt them long and destroy the memory of what they held most dear" (*Notes from Sick Rooms*, 240).

7

The Voyage Out

The Voyage Out, Virginia Woolf's first novel, is the one least read. Begun when she was twenty-five years old and revised many times before it was published, it is far less fluent than the book reviews and essays that had been appearing in print since she was twenty-two. "The first novel is always apt to be an unguarded one" (*Essays* 1:225), she wrote in one of those reviews—but her own first novel is surely an exception. Leonard Woolf, in his autobiography, recalls her discovering a mountain of discarded versions of the novel in a cupboard and burning them. But she had revised *The Voyage Out* so many times that the manuscripts she burned were not the only ones she had written. Others survive. And although the novel she published had been extensively reworked, the earlier versions are indeed unguarded: they point to what lies submerged beneath the published text.

Among the characters in *The Voyage Out* is a writer who declares that he is writing a novel about "silence, or the things that people do not say." His statement might serve as epigraph for *The Voyage Out*. The surviving manuscripts suggest what Virginia Woolf was trying both to say and to silence, in herself and in her first novel.

Flawed though it is, this first work of fiction has some passages that fairly leap off the page. The following is a speech Woolf gives to the writer, Terence Hewet, addressing the young woman who is the novel's central character. It is a passage Woolf might have written in her prime:

> Just consider: it's the beginning of the twentieth century, and until a few years ago no woman had

ever come out by herself and said things at all. There it was going on in the background, for all those thousands of years, this curious silent unrepresented life. Of course we're always writing about women—abusing them, or jeering at them, or worshipping them; but it's never come from women themselves. I believe we still don't know in the least how they live, or what they feel, or what they do precisely . . . It's the man's view that's represented, you see. (200)[1]

The speech that is here given to a male character would become the peroration of *A Room of One's Own* about the "infinitely obscure lives" of women that have gone unrecorded through history. He continues, "Think of a railway train: fifteen carriages for men who want to smoke. Doesn't it make your blood boil? If I were a woman I'd blow someone's brains out."

Hewet is addressing Rachel Vinrace, the novel's protagonist, who is twenty-four years old, a year younger than Woolf herself when she began working on the novel. Like Woolf, Rachel Vinrace is motherless, her mother having died when she was eleven. But unlike Woolf, she has read few books. She has been raised by her father's two sisters in Hampstead, where life has followed a routine that has kept Rachel sheltered. In her first novel Woolf sets this as-yet-unformed young woman on a sea voyage that takes her away from her familiar surroundings: Rachel leaves the

1. Citations throughout are to the Penguin edition of *The Voyage Out*, which reproduces the original version of the novel first published in England by Duckworth & Co. in 1915. Woolf continued to revise this novel even after it was published: in the first American edition, published by George H. Doran in 1920, substantial passages were cut. In 1929, when Leonard and Virginia Woolf's Hogarth Press published *The Voyage Out* in their Uniform Edition of her novels, she chose to reprint not the revised text, but the original version as it had first been published by Duckworth in 1915.

known world of England and travels to an exotic destination, a port on the coast of South America. The novel promises to be a bildungsroman, showing its protagonist's progress to maturity. When the protagonist is a woman, traditionally her growth would be reflected in the wise choice of a husband: marriage is the end toward which her development proceeds, and marriage is the culmination of the plot. *Persuasion* is an example: Jane Austen's novel is referred to several times in this one, and indeed a copy of *Persuasion* is placed in Rachel's hands. In her own first novel, Woolf directs the reader's attention to Austen's last.

Persuasion is also about a young woman, Anne Elliot, whose mother had died when she was thirteen. At eighteen, Anne rejected the marriage proposal of the man she loved, accepting the advice of her mother's dear friend, who cautioned her against marrying a man who had neither high birth nor fortune, but only his talents to recommend him: "She had been forced into prudence in her youth; she learned romance as she grew older." At twenty-seven, Anne Elliot is given the chance of making her decision again, and this time she accepts Captain Wentworth. The wisdom she has acquired in the intervening years is reflected in her choice of husband. No longer acquiescing to authority— that of a surrogate for the mother who died—Anne Elliot has come into possession of her own authority and now chooses the man whose intelligence, goodness, and maturity match her own. The novel that is placed in Rachel's hands exemplifies what literary convention has led us to expect.

But the plot of *The Voyage Out* leads not to the marriage of its heroine, but to her death. The ending of the book has always been problematic for readers. When the novel appeared, Lytton Strachey wrote to Woolf that "at the end I felt as if it was really only the beginning of an enormous novel, which had been—almost accidentally—cut short by the death of Rachel" (*Letters*, 55–56). Her death is given no convincing cause within the world of the novel. It seems to come from nowhere and has seemed to readers one of the novel's failings. Zwerdling (1986) writes of Rachel's illness and death as "a shocking betrayal of the conventions of the marriage plot the book seemed to accept" (p. 177). When Woolf began working on this novel, the recent marriage of Vanessa, following soon upon the death of Thoby, was very much on her mind, as was her sister's new motherhood. Now the four Stephens, who had formed a household in Bloomsbury after the death of their father, were reduced to two, Virginia and Adrian. She felt strongly the weight of expectation that she marry. In this "work of imagination," as she called it, she is contemplating the possibilities life offers a young woman. Marriage held terrors for her, and her first novel is at once an exploration and an enactment of those terrors.

The opening chapter is set in London, in the bustle of city streets. The first sentence is an observation that is also a warning to the reader: "As the streets that lead from the Strand to the Embankment are very narrow, it is better not to walk down them arm-in-arm." Mr. and Mrs. Ambrose, jostled by people and motor cars, begin arm-in-arm, but soon she withdraws:

> It was only by scorning all she met that she kept herself from tears, and the friction of people brushing past her was evidently painful. After watching the traffic on the Embankment for a minute or two with a stoical gaze she twitched her husband's sleeve, and they crossed between the swift discharge of motor cars. When they were safe on the further side, she gently withdrew her arm from his, allowing her mouth at the same time to relax, to tremble; then tears rolled down, and, leaning her elbows on the balustrade, she shielded her face from the curious. Mr. Ambrose attempted consolation; he patted her

shoulder; but she showed no signs of admitting him, and feeling it awkward to stand beside a grief that was greater than his, he crossed his arms behind him, and took a turn along the pavement. (3)

Quickly we are shown the tension within the couple. It is all done wordlessly, with shifts of feeling conveyed in the ballet of their gestures: the stoniness of her gaze, her twitching her husband's sleeve as they cross the street, the withdrawal of her arm, his patting her shoulder, and then, when she does not respond, crossing his arms behind him. Her struggle to contain her feelings is conveyed wholly in physical signs: as she allows her mouth to relax it trembles, then tears roll down. She rejects her husband's attempt at consolation, and he, for his part, withdraws too.

But when Mrs. Ambrose's tears come in spite of herself, her husband instantly breaks off the poem he has been reciting to himself and lays his hand upon her shoulder, calling her "dearest" in a supplicating tone: it is the first word that either speaks to the other. Momentarily the narrative point of view becomes that of the wife, who saw "the arches of Waterloo Bridge and the carts moving across them, like the line of animals in a shooting gallery" (5). She is estranged from her husband not only by grief but by rage.

The ballet of their gestures continues, suggesting the emotional currents between them without explanation—either to each other, or to the reader. When he hails a cab, she wants to walk; once he is too far away to hear her, she wants a cab. The wife seems almost willfully, perversely alone in her grief. That grief needs no explanation to her husband, and the narrator gives none to the reader. It will be some time before the cause of her grief is made known, that she is a mother leaving her children.

Helen and Ridley Ambrose board a small boat that carries

them out to the steamer *Euphrosyne*, the ship that will take them to South America. There, in a villa that awaits them, Mr. Ambrose plans to immerse himself in the translation of Pindar. On board the steamer they are greeted by Rachel Vinrace, who is their niece, and by Rachel's father, Willoughby Vinrace, captain of the *Euphrosyne*.

Whereas London had been melancholy, the sea air is wonderfully salty and brisk. The voyage begins happily with a soft blue sky and a calm sea. The reader is encouraged to have hopeful expectations: "They were free of roads, free of mankind, and the same exhilaration at their freedom ran through them all."

Stopping in Lisbon, they pick up two passengers, Mr. and Mrs. Dalloway, who had been traveling on the Continent for some weeks with a view to broadening Mr. Dalloway's mind. He is a member of Parliament, and he and his wife, Clarissa, are eager to increase their knowledge of the world: "In Spain he and Mrs. Dalloway had mounted mules, for they wished to understand how the peasants live." The picture of Richard Dalloway is a highly accomplished comic portrait. He is the quintessential public man, his conversation filled with rhetorical flourishes. Smug, self-satisfied, he cannot speak without holding forth. At dinner Helen Ambrose asks him whether he doesn't ever find it rather dull to be in Parliament:

> "If you ask me whether I ever find it rather dull," he said, "I am bound to say yes; on the other hand, if you ask me what career do you consider on the whole, taking the good with the bad, the most enjoyable and enviable, not to speak of its more serious side, of all careers, for a man, I am bound to say, 'The Politician's.' . . . All one's faculties have their play," said Richard. "I may be treading on dangerous ground; but what I feel about poets and arts in gen-

eral is this: on your own lines, you can't be beaten—
granted; but off your own lines—puff—one has to
make allowances. Now, I shouldn't like to think that
any one had to make allowances for me." (35–36)

Richard Dalloway proudly displays his disdain for the arts and
for artists, an attitude his wife shares. She adds that she herself likes it best when poets look like successful stockbrokers—
to which Helen Ambrose replies, sensibly enough, that there are
plenty of successful stockbrokers for Clarissa to look at.

Though he holds writers generally in contempt, Mr. Dalloway does approve of Jane Austen. He praises her for not attempting to write like a man, at the same time that he appropri-
ates her as "incomparably the greatest female writer we possess."
His esteem for Jane Austen does not prevent him, however, from
falling asleep while his wife reads aloud from *Persuasion*.

Richard Dalloway opposes extending the vote to women, and
he describes with annoyance having been incommoded by a suf-
fragist sitting on the steps of Parliament: "It was very awkward.
. . . At last I plucked up courage and said to her, 'My good creature, you're only in the way where you are. You're hindering me,
and you're doing no good to yourself.'" He pities suffragists for
the discomfort of sitting on those steps and concludes, "Nobody
can condemn the utter folly and futility of such behaviour more
than I do; and as for the whole agitation, well! may I be in my
grave before a woman has the right to vote in England! That's
all I say" (35). And closer to home, "I never allow my wife to talk
politics. . . . For this reason. It is impossible for human beings,
constituted as they are, both to fight and to have ideals. If I have
preserved mine, as I am thankful to say that in great measure I
have, it is due to the fact that I have been able to come home to
my wife in the evening and to find that she has spent her day in
calling, music, play with the children, domestic duties" (56). Sit-

ting next to Richard Dalloway at dinner, Rachel is quite taken by this pompous, pedestrian man. The banalities of his conversation are impressive to an impressionable young woman: mulling over what he had told her about himself, she thinks admiringly, "He had sisters and pets, and once lived in the country." Richard Dalloway is the first of the many men in this book who will tell Rachel what she should read: he will send her Burke, either the Speech on The French Revolution or The American Rebellion. (In fact, Burke's "Reflections on the Revolution in France" is in the form of a letter, not a speech. Dalloway makes errors when he is showing off.) Smug, pompous, philistine, disdainful of artists, patronizing toward women, Richard Dalloway is the type of all that Virginia Woolf held in contempt.

He is full of self-congratulation about his education, about his career, about his social class, about his marriage. And as soon as he is alone with Rachel, he seizes her and kisses her passionately. Rachel leaves her room quickly and goes out onto the deck of the ship. When she begins to put words to her experience, they are at first welcoming: "Life seemed to hold infinite possibilities she had never guessed at. She leant upon the rail and looked over the troubled grey waters where the sunlight was fitfully scattered upon the crests of the waves, until she was cold and absolutely calm again. Nevertheless something wonderful had happened" (67).

At dinner, however, she is disconcerted to find that she feels not "exalted," but uncomfortable. That night she has a dream whose tone contrasts with the "strange exultation" she felt just after the kiss:

> She was walking down a long tunnel, which grew
> so narrow by degrees that she could touch the damp
> bricks on either side. At length the tunnel opened
> and became a vault; she found herself trapped in it,

bricks meeting her wherever she turned, alone with a little deformed man who squatted on the floor gibbering, with long nails. His face was pitted and like the face of an animal. The wall behind him oozed with damp, which collected into drops and slid down. Still and cold as death she lay, not daring to move, until she broke the agony by tossing herself across the bed, and woke crying "Oh!" (68)

Waking, Rachel finds that the horror does not go at once: "She felt herself pursued, so that she got up and actually locked her door. A voice moaned for her, eyes desired her." The repellent sexuality of her dream is vivid in its physicality—in the damp, and the oozing, and the drops sliding. The long tunnel that opens into a vault oozing with damp is obviously suggestive of female sexuality. The terror of being the object of men's lust is conveyed within the dream by the deformed little man with whom she is trapped, and in waking life, in vivid synecdoche, by voices moaning for her and eyes desiring her.

The kiss, which at first had made Rachel feel that life holds infinite possibilities, prompts a dream in which sexuality is repugnant and dangerous. Even after the dream, however, Rachel could still say to Helen, in rapid succession, both that "Men are brutes! I hate men!" and also that "I liked him, and I liked being kissed."

The kiss itself has repercussions that go beyond the physical experience. The recognition that as a woman she is the object of men's lust causes Rachel to see the whole of her life differently than she had before. She sees, now, that her sexual vulnerability limits her freedom. Her aunt Helen, older and more worldly, tries to get Rachel to treat the matter more lightly. "It's the most natural thing in the world," she tells her. "Men will want to kiss you, just as they'll want to marry you. The pity is to get things out of proportion." But Rachel is not mollified. "Her mind was working," we are told, "very quickly, inconsistently and painfully." Finally she burst out, "'So that's why I can't walk alone!'

"By this new light she saw her life for the first time a creeping hedged-in thing, driven cautiously between high walls, here turned aside, there plunged in darkness, made dull and crippled for ever—her life that was the only chance she had" (72). Woolf gives her young protagonist an interior monologue of some eloquence and urgency. If men are lustful and predatory and women vulnerable, women cannot move about the world freely, cannot venture out alone: they are compelled to live lives that are cramped and diminished.

Rachel's first kiss, setting off a tumult of contradictory feelings, shakes loose her customary ways of seeing herself. Having served this narrative purpose, the Dalloways disembark at an unspecified shore, but not before Clarissa Dalloway has given Rachel her copy of *Persuasion* as a parting gift. Again Woolf directs the reader's attention to Austen's last novel, with its promise of marriage as the fulfillment of the heroine's life.

Talking about the Dalloways with Helen Ambrose, Rachel vacillates between thinking that perhaps she was taken in and thinking that it was a large and interesting world she had glimpsed. What is told of Rachel's development prior to this point in the narrative? She had been educated

> as the majority of well-to-do girls in the last part
> of the nineteenth century were educated. . . . There
> was no subject in the world which she knew accurately. Her mind was in the state of an intelligent
> man's in the beginning of the reign of Queen Elizabeth. . . . The shape of the earth, the history of the

world, how trains worked, or money was invested, what laws were in force, which people wanted what, and why they wanted it, the most elementary idea of a system in modern life—none of this had been imparted to her by any of her professors or mistresses. But this system of education had one great advantage. It did not teach anything, but it put no obstacle in the way of any real talent that the pupil might chance to have. Rachel, being musical, was allowed to learn nothing but music; she became a fanatic about music. All the energies that might have gone into languages, science, or literature, that might have made her friends, or shown her the world, poured straight into music. (26)

Woolf gave Rachel the sort of haphazard education she felt herself to have had, and she gave her too, as she had been given, a talent which, "as became daily more obvious, was a really generous allowance."

Alone in her room on board the ship, Rachel picks up one book, then another, without interest. First she picks up a translation of Tristan and then, throwing that down, picks up Cowper's *Letters*, which had been prescribed for her by her father. This too bores her, but the mention of the smell of broom in Cowper's garden awakens a memory of her own: she saw the little hall at Richmond laden with flowers on the day of her mother's funeral,

> smelling so strong that now any flower-scent brought back the sickly horrible sensation; and so from one scene she passed, half-hearing, half-seeing, to another. She saw her Aunt Lucy arranging flowers in the drawing-room.

"Aunt Lucy," she volunteered, "I don't like the smell of broom; it reminds me of funerals."

"Nonsense, Rachel," Aunt Lucy replied; "don't say such foolish things, dear. I always think it a particularly cheerful plant." (28)

Her memories are stirred, in Proustian fashion, by a sensory experience, a smell: the smell of broom mentioned by Cowper, the smell of the flowers on the day of her mother's funeral, the smell of the broom her aunt Lucy was arranging in the drawing room. This brief memory suggests a great deal about her life with her aunts: the dismissal of her memories, of her experience, of her feelings. "Nonsense," her aunt says, insisting that cheerfulness be substituted for sorrow. Deflecting Rachel's allusion to the death of her mother, her aunt silences her.

Growing up in this household, Rachel learned that "to feel anything strongly was to create an abyss between oneself and others who feel strongly perhaps but differently. It was far better to play the piano and forget all the rest. . . . It appeared that nobody ever said a thing they meant, or talked of a feeling they felt, but that was what music was for" (29). Silence enfolds the death of Rachel's mother and indeed all that "one saw and felt." Her art is the only refuge from loneliness and from rage: "Absorbed by her music she accepted her lot very complacently, blazing into indignation perhaps once a fortnight, and subsiding as she subsided now."

On her sea journey, too, Rachel turns to the piano when she is overcome by a sense of loss. At one point Clarissa and Helen begin to talk about children and relax into a tone of greater cordiality. Rachel becomes "indignant with the prosperous matrons, who made her feel outside their world and motherless." She leaves them abruptly, slams the door of her room, and pulls out her music:

In three minutes she was deep in a very difficult, very classical fugue in A, and over her face came a queer remote impersonal expression of complete absorption and anxious satisfaction. Now she stumbled; now she faltered and had to play the same bar twice over, but an invisible line seemed to string the notes together, from which rose a shape, a building. She was so far absorbed in this work, for it was really difficult to find how all these sounds should stand together, and drew upon the whole of her faculties, that she never heard a knock at the door. (48–49)

Rachel finds in her art a refuge from grief and rage and pain. The particular imagery of this passage anticipates the terms that Woolf would use many years later, in her memoir, to describe the transformative power of her own art. For Rachel there is an invisible line stringing the notes together, and the difficulty is to find how all these sounds should stand together. For Woolf it is through language that she somehow puts the "severed parts" together, creating a whole:

I feel that I have had a blow; but it is not, as I thought as a child, simply a blow from an enemy hidden behind the cotton wool of daily life; it is or will become a revelation of some order; it is a token of some real thing behind appearances; and I make it real by putting it into words. *It is only by putting it into words that I make it whole; this wholeness means that it has lost its power to hurt me;* it gives me, perhaps because by doing so I take away the pain, a great delight to *put the severed parts together.* ("A Sketch of the Past," 72; emphasis added)

It is not at all clear what "severed parts" Woolf is referring to. Severed parts of what? The phrase has no referent, even in the fuller context of the memoir, which I quoted in chapter 3. But when this passage is placed alongside the passage from her first novel, together they suggest that for Virginia Woolf the consoling power of art has to do with putting elements together, whether words or sounds, as a way to overcome separation and loss.

Helen Ambrose is dismayed to discover how little her niece knows, and she undertakes to educate her. She proposes that once they reach South America, instead of continuing up the Amazon with her father, Rachel remain with her and Ridley in their villa. The villa they have rented is in Santa Marina, within sight of a small hotel that houses a colony of English people. These, then, are the people who make up Rachel's social world, who personify the range of possibilities the author offers her. Each reflects in some way upon the question of marriage. There are two married couples, the Thornburys and the Elliots. The Thornburys, brimming with self-satisfaction, are the parents of eleven children. They have sons in the army and the navy, and their "baby" is at Cambridge. When mail arrives from England, the wife reads aloud to her husband, with approving commentary, the trivial details of their children's lives. The other married couple are the Elliots; Hughling Elliot is an Oxford don. When we meet them, Mrs. Elliot is waiting in bed for her husband: "How late you are, Hugh! . . . You know I never can sleep when I'm waiting for you"—to which her husband makes no reply. This is a portrait of marriage as peevish dependency. Mrs. Elliot is a woman whose expression is habitually plaintive: it is an astute characterization of a woman who is chronically depressed and who finds cause for depression wherever she looks. When the subject of dogs comes up, she embarks on a long, sad history of a wire-haired terrier owned by an uncle of hers which had committed suicide. She finds a flat country so depressing; she pities the queen of Holland, who has had a baby daughter after eight childless years of marriage. When the conversation turns to women giving birth on ships, Mrs. Elliot says, "We've got a lot to complain of!" Above all, she sighs over her own childlessness.

As the guests gather after breakfast to read the *Times*, Woolf stages a conversation between these two married women, one with many children, one childless, about another guest, Miss Allan, a woman who is not married. Miss Allan is engaged in writing a short "Primer of English Literature, Beowulf to Swinburne." When we meet her, she is alone in her room at night reading Wordsworth's "Prelude"; after breakfast, she looks anxiously at the time and goes back to her room to work. Mrs. Thornbury and Mrs. Elliot watch her withdraw, a "square figure in its manly coat." Miss Allan is frequently described, by the other characters and by the narrator, as being like a man and as having a careworn face: "'And I'm sure she has a hard life,' sighed Mrs. Elliot.

'Oh, it is a hard life,' said Mrs. Thornbury. 'Unmarried women —earning their livings—it's the hardest life of all.'

'Yet she seems pretty cheerful,' said Mrs. Elliot.

'It must be very interesting,' said Mrs. Thornbury. 'I envy her her knowledge.'

'But that isn't what women want,' said Mrs. Elliot" (104). Mrs. Elliot describes herself as a woman who knows what it is to be childless. "I sketch a great deal . . . but that isn't really an occupation."

The older women at the hotel represent an array of possibilities that is either foolish, or grim, or poignant. What of the young women? When we meet Susan Warrington, she is brushing her hair and assessing herself in the mirror, wondering what

Arthur Venning thinks of her looks. Susan's life as a young single woman is spent in servitude to her elderly aunt, Mrs. Paley, who is querulous and demanding. When Arthur Venning does propose to her, and Susan becomes not a single woman but an engaged woman, her aunt begins to treat her with more respect. There is another unmarried young woman at the hotel, Evelyn Murgatroyd, an unappealing character who accosts her fellow guests in an aggressive fashion, reveals too much about herself, and is preoccupied with getting married. She asks repeatedly which of two marriage proposals she should accept, but it is clear that the decision is arbitrary. One man would do just as well as the other.

Two other guests at the hotel, the writer Terence Hewet and his friend St. John Hirst, will be central to the narrative. We are introduced to these men in a scene in which Hewet comes to his friend's room and finds him engrossed in reading Gibbon's *History of the Decline and Fall of the Roman Empire:* "A whole procession of splendid sentences entered his capacious brow and went marching through his brain in order." Hewet proposes that they organize an expedition for the purpose of bringing together the guests of the hotel. It would be nice, he adds, to take along something to read, should they get tired of looking at the view. He suggests "Modern Love," a poem sequence by George Meredith that describes the dissolution of a happy marriage, and along the same lines he quotes the closing stanza of Thomas Hardy's "He Abjures Love." An odd, discordant note is struck without being integrated into the text. In a mood that is seemingly energetic and optimistic, plans are made for the excursion.

These two young men, taking books on their picnic, will, like most of the men in this novel, undertake to educate Rachel, to tell her what she must read. What does she herself choose to read? One of the promises Helen Ambrose had made, if she stayed with them, was a room of her own, large and private: "a room in which she could play, read, think, defy the world, a fortress as well as a sanctuary." Indeed, "when she shut the door Rachel entered an enchanted place, where the poets sang and things fell into their right proportions." Absorbed in her reading, she feels herself to be "an heroic statue in the middle of the foreground, dominating the view. Ibsen's plays always left her in that condition" (112). The play is not named, but the heroine is: Nora, who in the end leaves the doll's house of her marriage. And another literary heroine is named: we are told that after acting Ibsen for days at a time, "then it would be Meredith's turn and she became Diana of the Crossways."

Rachel's identification with characters in books and plays suggests a more lively engagement with literature than is apparent when the men in this novel instruct her in what she ought to read. The heroine of George Meredith's novel is mentioned once, and the narrative moves on, but the allusion is significant. In *A Room of One's Own*, Woolf credits Meredith, in *Diana of the Crossways*, with one of the few attempts to portray in fiction a friendship between two women. Indeed, the friendship between Diana and Lady Dunstane is the richest, most sustaining relationship in the novel. Diana does marry, but her first marriage nearly destroys her, and it is only by earning her own living—as a writer—that she is able to save herself. After her husband dies, some twists and turns of the plot lead to a more promising second marriage.

But Meredith gives his heroine deep misgivings about marriage. As a young woman she treasures her liberty, seeing in the unmarried state the greatest freedom of mind. She says to her friend Lady Dunstane, "I cannot tell you what a foreign animal a husband would appear in my kingdom":

> Her experience had awakened a sexual aversion, of
> some slight kind, enough to make her feminine

pride stipulate for perfect independence, that she might have the calm out of which imagination spreads wing. Imagination had become her broader life, and on such an earth, under such skies, a husband who is not the fountain of them certainly is a foreign animal: he is a discordant note. He contracts the ethereal world, deadens radiancy. He is gross fact, a leash, a muzzle, harness, a hood, whatever is detestable to the free limbs and senses. (*Diana of the Crossways*, 48–49)

Like Diana, Rachel figures man as animal, both in the dream that followed her first kiss and again in a hallucination toward the end of the novel. But a husband would do more than just intrude his animal nature; he would limit the freedom of her mind. Thus the reading that Woolf gives her heroine tacitly subverts the marriage plot; it undercuts the promise of the voyage out.

The subject of books—of education—is one of the central themes of this novel. Repeatedly the reader is reminded that history, philosophy, literature belong to men: to Mr. Dalloway, to Willoughby Vinrace, to Ridley Ambrose and Terence Hewet and St. John Hirst, even to a man who does not appear directly in the novel, the brother of Helen Ambrose. As the characters introduce themselves to one another, Helen Ambrose states her father's occupation and adds that he had gone bankrupt, "for which reason she had never been properly educated." An elder brother, she says, had lent her books. Similarly, Rachel, asked to give a sketch of herself, says that her father is a shipowner and adds that she "had never been properly educated."

Books belong to men and are theirs to give or, more precisely, to lend. Men feel themselves entitled to this heritage, even when the books have been written by women: Richard Dalloway declares with his customary self-congratulation that Jane Austen is "the finest female writer *we possess*" (emphasis added). Rachel has books recommended to her and lent to her by most of the men in the novel. But it is only a woman, Clarissa Dalloway, who actually gives her a book, placing in Rachel's hands her copy of *Persuasion* as a parting gift.

If Mr. Dalloway embodies masculine self-importance of the political type, St. John Hirst embodies masculine self-importance of the academic type: "At Cambridge, of course, I should inevitably become the most important man in the place." At one point in their conversation Rachel ventures to tell him that she plays the piano very well, but Hirst shows no interest. It is clear to him that she has "obviously never thought or felt or seen anything," and he begins to quiz her about what she has read. Rachel is slightly annoyed by his manner, but nonetheless "his masculine acquirements induced her to take a very modest view of her own power." He, on his side, aggressively persists: "You see, the problem is, can one really talk to you? Have you got a mind, or are you like the rest of your sex?" Having declared that he will lend her his Gibbon, he makes no bones about the fact that it is a test to see whether she can appreciate Gibbon: "It's awfully difficult to tell about women . . . how much, I mean, is due to lack of training, and how much is native incapacity."

Rachel's "slight annoyance" soon turns into tears of rage. She declares vehemently to Terence Hewet that Hirst has made her furious with his insolence, but when Hewet expresses surprise, she quickly retreats: "I dare say I'm a fool." She could not explain "why Hirst's assumption of the superiority of his nature and experience had seemed to her not only galling but terrible — as if a gate had clanged in her face." Pacing up and down beside Hewet, Rachel declares bitterly, "It's no good; we should live separate; we cannot understand each other; we only bring out what's worst." Hirst's arrogance makes her long for a world of women alone: "She would be a Persian princess far from civilization, riding her horse upon the mountains alone, and making her women sing to her in the evening, far from all this, from the strife of men and women" (142).

There is a scene in her first novel that will recur as a topos in Woolf's writing. A diffident young woman ventures into the library of a scholar, where she feels herself to be—and is treated as—an outsider, a stranger. The scholar is older, and male, and fully at home in the heritage of Western civilization arrayed upon his shelves. It is Cam entering the library of Mr. Ramsay in *To the Lighthouse*, it is Woolf as she describes herself, age fifteen, entering the library of her father. Here it is Rachel, venturing into the study of her uncle, Ridley Ambrose, who is engaged in translating Pindar. She has come to borrow a book, and he speaks to her in a way that intensifies her sense of being an outsider: "But what's the use of reading if you don't read Greek? After all, if you read Greek, you need never read anything else, pure waste of time." The verbs position them in relation to one another: Rachel "stammered" and "confessed"; her uncle "demanded" and "exclaimed."

Rachel has come to ask if she may borrow Gibbon, which Hirst has directed her to read. Her uncle ridicules her request: "I don't travel about with a miscellaneous collection of eighteenth century historians! Gibbon! Ten big volumes at least." Rachel apologizes for interrupting and turns to go, but he stops her, puts down his pipe, and leads her around the room, naming the authors on his shelves. He tells her she should read Balzac, and in the end she asks either for Balzac or for the Speech on the American Revolution, which Mr. Dalloway had recommended. "Good Lord!" is his response, and he proceeds to patronize her by quizzing her on the dance, which he presumes is the only thing of interest to her, all the while expressing his own contempt for it.

The arrogance of men—and the diffidence of women in acquiescing to that arrogance—are the subject of a fascinating passage of analysis. It is a speech that Woolf gives to Terence Hewet about "the respect that women, even well-educated, very able women, have for men":

> I believe we must have the sort of power over you that we're said to have over horses. They see us three times as big as we are or they'd never obey us. For that very reason, I'm inclined to doubt that you'll ever do anything even when you have the vote. . . . It'll take six generations before you're sufficiently thick-skinned to go into law courts and business offices. Consider what a bully the ordinary man is . . . the ordinary hard-working, rather ambitious solicitor or man of business with a family to bring up. . . . Of course, the daughters have to give way to the sons; the sons have to be educated; they have to bully and shove for their wives and families, and so it all comes over again. And meanwhile there are the women in the background. . . . Do you really think that the vote will do you any good? (196)

Written when Woolf herself did not yet have the right to vote, it is a passage of remarkable prescience.

The ways in which men and women act toward one another are forged in families, and it is in families that they are replicated from one generation to the next. Sons learn to have a sense of entitlement and to be aggressive in pursuit of what they feel entitled to; daughters learn to be deferential. Daughters who give way to sons grow up to be wives who give way to husbands: and for this reason these habits will take generations to alter.

Woolf addresses here not only the question of why men are bullies, but of why women allow themselves to be bullied. It is in families, she argues, that men learn their own importance and the importance of their activities, while women learn their own triviality. The character traits of women and men—the habits, respectively, of deference and entitlement—are bred in the family, and it is in the family that these traits are carried on from generation to generation.

Alone among the men in this novel, Terence Hewet asks Rachel to tell him about herself. Men, he recognizes, can know little about women: "If one's a man, the only confidences one gets are from young women about their love affairs. But the lives of women of forty, of unmarried women, of working women, of women who keep shops and bring up children, of women like your aunts or Mrs. Thornbury or Miss Allan—one knows nothing whatever about them. They won't tell you. Either they're afraid, or they've got a way of treating men" (200). Hewet presses Rachel to tell him about her life at home. "Imagine it's a Wednesday and you're all at luncheon," he says to her, arranging three pebbles on the grass to represent Rachel, Aunt Lucy, and Aunt Clara. And he expresses interest in her art: "What I want to do in writing novels is very much what you want to do when you play the piano, I expect. . . . We want to find out what's behind things, don't we."

At only one point in the novel does Rachel's music come out of her room and become something other than her private refuge. To celebrate the engagement of Susan Warrington and Arthur Venning, a dance is held. Toward the end of the evening, suddenly the music stops in spite of couples who were imploring the musicians for one more dance. As Rachel turns over the sheets of music that lie on the piano, she remarks, "No wonder they get sick of playing stuff like this, they're really hymn tunes, played very fast, with bits out of Wagner and Beethoven." At this point the guests turn to her: from all sides her gift for playing the piano is insisted upon, and at last Rachel has to consent.

At the piano Rachel shows herself to be knowledgeable, self-assured, and resourceful. First she plays the only pieces of dance music she can remember, and then she goes on to play an air from a sonata by Mozart. When one of the guests protests that it's not a dance, she replies, "It is: invent the steps," and "sure of her melody she marked the rhythm boldly so as to simplify the way." From Mozart, "Rachel passed without stopping to old English hunting songs, carols, and hymn tunes, for, as she had observed, any good tune, with a little management, became a tune one could dance to. By degrees every person in the room was tripping and turning in pairs or alone" (152). In their exuberance they dance the night away, until the older people begin to make their way up to bed: "Rachel, though robbed of her audience, had gone on playing to herself. From John Peel she passed to Bach, who was at this time the subject of her intense enthusiasm, and one by one some of the younger dancers came in from the garden and sat upon the deserted gilt chairs round the piano. . . . As they sat and listened, their nerves were quieted; the heat and soreness of their lips, the result of incessant talking and laughing, was smoothed away" (153).

In her music Rachel shows herself more forceful, more imaginative, more inventive than at any other point in the novel. Yet Woolf seems uncertain what to do with Rachel's art. It all but disappears from the narrative after this display. Her art serves as a refuge for Rachel, but it does not lead in any way to the future or expand the array of alternatives offered her in the world of this novel.

Terence asks himself whether he is in love with Rachel and, having put the question into words, begins to think about marriage. A series of unpleasant pictures presents itself to his mind. He thinks of married friends at home and of the various couples at the hotel, Susan Warrington and Arthur Venning, the Thornburys, the Elliots, the Ambroses: "Was not their marriage too a compromise? She gave way to him; she spoilt him; she arranged things for him; she who was all truth to others was not true to her husband, was not true to her friends if they came in conflict with her husband" (229). He tried out pictures of married couples in his mind's eye, but he saw them always "walled up in a warm firelit room." When he began to think of unmarried people, however, "he saw them active in an unlimited world; . . . All the most individual and humane of his friends were bachelors and spinsters; indeed he was surprised to find that the women he most admired and knew best were unmarried women. Marriage seemed to be worse for them than it was for men" (228). It would be difficult not to read the interior monologue given to Terence as Woolf's own grim view—at a point in her life when she was herself a marriageable young woman, writing and rewriting her novel about a marriageable young woman.

Terence continues, addressing Rachel in his imagination: "I worship you, but I loathe marriage, I hate its smugness, its safety, its compromise, and the thought of you interfering in my work, hindering me." And then his thoughts turn: "'Oh you're free!' he exclaimed, in exultation at the thought of her, 'and I'd keep you free. We'd be free together.'"

A text which bears further on this troubling matter is emphatically, but elliptically, cited. As St. John Hirst and Terence Hewet arrive at church service one Sunday morning, attention is drawn to the thin book bound in light blue cloth which Hirst carries under his arm instead of a black prayer book. During the service he reads steadily in the volume, while Mrs. Flushing, seated next to him, leans closer to get a better look. Hirst lays the book before her: "Sappho. The one Swinburne did— the best thing that's ever been written."

This protracted bit of stage business directs the reader's attention to the book; Mrs. Flushing's response underscores the importance it is meant to have. She "gulped down the Ode to Aphrodite during the Litany, keeping herself with difficulty from asking when Sappho lived, and what else she wrote worth reading, and contriving to come in punctually at the end with 'the forgiveness of sins, the Resurrection of the body, and the life everlasting. Amen.'" Hirst takes pleasure in flouting the forced solemnity of the church. Indeed, at lunch Hewet accuses him of ostentation: why go to church, he asks, merely in order to read Sappho?

The poem that Hirst brings into the service is referred to as the "Ode to Aphrodite," but the title does not have a clear referent. Schlack (1979) suggests that Woolf may mean Swinburne's "On the Cliffs," which begins with a Greek line from Sappho and renders some of her fragments within its text; or perhaps Swinburne's "Anactoria," which is also prefaced by a Greek quote from Sappho. I believe, however, that Woolf's allusion is to "Sapphics," which is the only Swinburne poem that specifically mentions Aphrodite.

In this poem Sappho, as the speaker, describes a vision that comes to her as she lies awake all night. The goddess Aphrodite calls to her: "Turn to me, O my Sappho." But instead, Sappho turns toward the Lesbian women. She

> saw the Lesbians kissing across their smitten
> Lutes with lips more sweet than the sound of
>   lute-strings,
> Mouth to mouth and hand upon hand, her chosen,
>   Fairer than all men;
>
> Only saw the beautiful lips and fingers,
> Full of songs and kisses and little whispers,
> Full of music; only beheld among them
>   Soar, as a bird soars

Newly fledged, her visible song, a marvel,
Made of perfect sound and exceeding passion,
Sweetly shapen, terrible, full of thunders,
    Clothed with the bird's wings.

Then rejoiced she, laughing with love, and scattered
Roses, awful roses of holy blossom;
Then the Loves thronged sadly with hidden faces
    Round Aphrodite . . .

In turning to the Lesbian women, Sappho makes a joyful choice, but one that is terrible in its consequence. The Muses are stricken silent, and even the gods grow pale. All flee from Sappho "with a fresh repulsion" and leave the land "barren, / Full of fruitless women and music only":

Unbeloved, unseen in the ebb of twilight,
Ghosts of outcast women return lamenting,
    Purged not in Lethe,

Clothed about with flame and with tears, and singing
Songs that move the heart of the shaken heaven,
Songs that break the heart of the earth with pity,
    Hearing, to hear them.

At the point Rachel and Terence fall in love, Woolf inserts into the narrative, with much emphasis, a reference to a poem that is explicitly about choosing between the love of men and the love of women. In the poem, Sappho chooses to turn away from Aphrodite and her entreaties, and embraces instead the love of the Lesbian women. The consequences of that choice are disastrous.

    After the scene in church with its subversive allusion to Sappho, Rachel is invited by the two unmarried women in the novel, first Evelyn Murgatroyd and then Miss Allan, to visit them in their rooms. Evelyn wants to talk about the two proposals of marriage she has received. One of the men caught her and kissed her: "The disgusting brute—I can still feel his nasty hairy face just there—" And she continues, "They've no dignity, they've no courage, they've nothing but their beastly passions and their brute strength!" After she flees from Evelyn, Rachel is invited to Miss Allan's room: having been reminded of the brutishness of men, she looks into the life of a woman alone. Miss Allan's face, we are told, was "much lined with care and thought." The writing table was piled with manuscript, and on the armchair were two heaps of library books, with slips of paper sticking out. Unlike a man, who is fully at home in his library—Ridley Ambrose, who proudly displays on his shelves the books he owns—Miss Allan appears ill at ease among the books she uses. These books are not her own but are borrowed from the library. She seems diffident, anxious about her task, which is laborious rather than heartfelt. "'Age of Chaucer, Age of Elizabeth, Age of Dryden,' she reflected; 'I'm glad there aren't many more ages.'" She asks Rachel to help her with a tiresome set of hooks on her dress, which, she says, "I *can* fasten for myself, but it takes from ten to fifteen minutes, whereas with your help—" The small request she makes of her young friend suggests, briefly, sparely, the hardness of a life alone.

Between her visits to the rooms of the two women, Rachel walks down a passage to a window, from which she looks down on the kitchen premises, "the wrong side of hotel life." What she encounters is a repellent and vividly imagined scene, bloody and terrible, a scene of casual violence by women:

> Two large women in cotton dresses were sitting on a
> bench with blood-smeared tin trays in front of them
> and yellow bodies across their knees. They were

plucking the birds, and talking as they plucked. Suddenly a chicken came floundering, half flying, half running into the space, pursued by a third woman whose age could hardly be under eighty. Although wizened and unsteady on her legs she kept up the chase, egged on by the laughter of the others; her face was expressive of furious rage, and as she ran she swore in Spanish. Frightened by hand-clapping here, a napkin there, the bird ran this way and that in sharp angles, and finally sluttered straight at the old woman, who opened her scanty grey skirts to enclose it, dropped upon it in a bundle, and then holding it out cut its head off with an expression of vindictive energy and triumph combined. (238–39)

The physicality of the women is emphasized: the yellow bodies of the chickens slung across the knees of the two large women, who are plucking the birds while talking; the old woman who opens her scanty grey skirts to enclose the chicken whose head she will cut off. We are told that "the blood and the ugly wriggling fascinated Rachel." Both fascinating and repellent, the scene in the courtyard is a tableau of violence by women; it is interposed between scenes which give Rachel a glimpse into the lives of the two women who are not married. In the ugliness and naked aggression of the scene in the courtyard, it seems as though a nightmare were breaking through the surface of the narrative.

At this point in the narrative, significantly, Rachel begins to experience the first symptoms of her illness. What is called in the novel Rachel's fever, the illness that will lead to her death, is first anticipated here, after she witnesses the violent scene of the women in the courtyard. She is agitated; her eyes "dazed by tears, she indulged herself at last in violent abuse of the entire day." She disliked everything she saw, "all things were wrong, all people stupid." Finally, her sense of reality falters: "'It's a dream,' she murmured . . . 'We're asleep and dreaming,' she repeated. . . . She was no longer able to see the world as a town laid out beneath her. It was covered instead by a haze of feverish red mist." Rachel experiences sudden perceptual changes. A group of people at the hotel "appeared with startling intensity, as though the dusty surface had been peeled off everything." She takes a violent dislike to Susan Warrington, the woman whose engagement was the occasion of the dance, who until this point has seemed innocuous. Now "she appeared insincere and cruel; she saw her grown stout and prolific, the kind blue eyes now shallow and watery, the bloom of the cheeks congealed to a network of dry red canals." In this state Rachel suddenly turns against Helen with some vehemence: "Thank God, Helen, I'm not like you! I sometimes think you don't think or feel or care or do anything but exist! . . . You're only half alive." Helen thinks she understands the reason for the outburst: Rachel was in love, "and she pitied her profoundly."

It is proposed that a group undertake a journey upriver by boat, a journey of about five days, to see a native village before they return to England. This journey away from the familiar landmarks of civilization is the context in which Terence and Rachel declare their love. The steamer pulls alongside the riverbank, the small boat they are towing is brought to the side, and as the other passengers settle on the bank of the river, Terence and Rachel decide to walk into the woods together. The setting is strange and ominous:

> As they passed into the depths of the forest the light grew dimmer, and the noises of the ordinary world were replaced by those creaking and sighing sounds

which suggest to the traveller in a forest that he is walking at the bottom of the sea. The path narrowed and turned; it was hedged in by dense creepers which knotted tree to tree, and burst here and there into star-shaped crimson blossoms. The sighing and creaking up above were broken every now and then by the jarring cry of some startled animal. (256)

They declare their love for each other in dialogue that is as strange and ominous as the setting. "You like being with me?" Terence asks. "Yes, with you," she replies.

From the moment that love is spoken of, Rachel's voice takes on an automaton-like quality. "We are happy together," Terence says. "Very happy," she answers. "'We love each other,' Terence said. 'We love each other,' she repeated."

As they declare their love, Rachel's speech echoes his, expressionless and empty. When she touches his face, Terence is overcome by a sense of unreality:

> This body of his was unreal; the whole world was unreal.
>
> "What's happened?" he began. "Why did I ask you to marry me? How did it happen?"
>
> "Did you ask me to marry you?" she wondered. They faded far away from each other, and neither of them could remember what had been said.
>
> "We sat upon the ground," he recollected.
>
> "We sat upon the ground," she confirmed him. (267)

They set out to rejoin the others, and Terence is at first unable to find the way back. Rachel's movements, like her words, simply repeat his. She follows him, stopping where he stops, turning where he turns, without knowing why he stopped or why he turned.

Rachel and Terence have been transformed on an instant. They speak differently; they act differently. The abrupt discontinuity is a significant flaw in the novel. Perhaps the sudden change may be understood as the reflection of Woolf's own fears of losing her individuality in marriage, of losing her voice. But it may also be understood as an attempt to find refuge from her fears—for this "love," in its echoings and mirrorings, obliterates the difference between man and woman. As Rachel echoes Terence's words, there is an absence of sexual polarity, even of sexual difference between them: "Simultaneously they stopped, clasped each other in their arms, then, releasing themselves, dropped to the earth" (257). The curious syntax of this sentence seems designed to avoid the singular and to avoid the gendered pronouns "he" and "she." Rachel and Terence "speak with one voice," asking Helen whether she did not think them the happiest people she had ever known.

While the characters rely upon platitudes to assure themselves of their happiness, Woolf attributes to both of them psychotic-like experiences—suddenly altering states of consciousness, feelings of unreality, cognitive faltering. Indeed at this point the narrative itself falters, and there is a puzzling, disturbing passage that breaks the surface of the fiction: it is an important passage to which I shall return after following the novel to its conclusion.

Having initially expressed an interest in Rachel's music, Terence now interrupts her piano playing and disparages the late Beethoven sonata she has been working on, preferring "nice simple tunes" that would be helpful to his literary composition. In contrast to his earlier promise that they would be "free together" he now tells her irritably, handing her some letters, "We're wasting the morning—I ought to be writing my book, and you ought to be answering these." It is clear that in marriage Rachel will be subsumed and absorbed by her husband—and that her art will be lost.

Now Terence joins the ranks of men who take it upon themselves to instruct Rachel in what to read: "God, Rachel, you do read trash! . . . No one dreams of reading this kind of thing now—antiquated problem plays, harrowing descriptions of life in the East End—oh, no, we've exploded all that. Read poetry, Rachel, poetry, poetry, poetry!" (275). He stops being curious about her; instead he claims to know her. What he "knows" is a contemptuous stereotype: "With all your virtues you don't and you never will, care with every fibre of your being for the pursuit of truth! You've no respect for facts, Rachel; you're essentially feminine." As he continues to criticize and patronize and provoke her, he finally declares, "Now you look as if you'd blow my brains out." He continues, "There are moments when, if we stood on a rock together, you'd throw me into the sea." Rachel starts to echo him mechanically, "If we stood on a rock together . . . ," and then the narrative shifts to her point of view: "To be flung into the sea, to be washed hither and thither, and driven about the roots of the world—the idea was incoherently delightful" (281).

Whereas earlier Terence had shown his interest by pressing Rachel to tell him particulars about her life, now it is he who talks and she who listens: "But he had known many more people, and was far more highly skilled in the art of narrative than Rachel was, whose experiences were, for the most part, of a curiously childlike and humourous kind, so that it generally fell to her lot to listen and ask questions" (282).

The man who had spoken passionately about the "curious, silent, unrepresented life of women" has become smug and tyrannical, dismissive of Rachel's art, dismissive of Rachel herself. The transformation happens from the moment that Terence and Rachel declare their love for one another.

Having set her twenty-four-year-old heroine on a sea voyage that takes her away from the familiar world of England to an exotic landscape, Woolf has led us to expect that Rachel will mature and make choices that reflect her maturity and shape her future. But this the author cannot give her. Marriage would destroy Rachel's individuality. And it would force the issue of sexuality, which has been repellent each time it shows its animal face. But what alternative is there to marriage within the world of the novel? Eroticism between women held its own terrors. The life of a woman alone, even an educated woman, is shown to be pinched and cramped, lined with care. Rachel has an art, her music, and like the author a large measure of talent, but Woolf seems to have little conviction that these alter the range of possibilities for a young woman.

In the end Woolf moves her heroine not toward marriage but to death. Rachel's fatal illness is given no name; it has no cause within the world of the novel. Its symptoms, however, are familiar: they are Woolf's own. The onset of Rachel's illness is signaled by a headache—as were Woolf's episodes of psychosis. Her headache begins at a point in the narrative when Terence is reading aloud to her. The words he read

> sounded strange; they meant different things from what they usually meant. Rachel at any rate could not keep her attention fixed upon them, but went off upon curious trains of thought suggested by words such as 'curb' and 'Locrine' and 'Brute,' which brought unpleasant sights before her eyes, independently of their meaning. Owing to the heat and the dancing air the garden too looked strange—the

trees were either too near or too far, and her head
almost certainly ached. (308–09)

As Rachel's head begins to ache, Terence is reading aloud from
Milton's *Comus* the song invoking Sabrina, calling on her to
come and save the Lady whose virtue is endangered by the lustful
Comus:

> Sabrina fair,
>   Listen where thou art sitting
> Under the glassy, cool, translucent wave,
>   In twisted braids of lilies knitting
> The loose train of thy amber dropping hair,
> Listen for dear honour's sake,
>   Goddess of the silver lake,
>   Listen and save!

In Comus's crystal glass is a potion that can change the human
countenance

> Into some brutish form of Wolf, or Bear,
> Or Ounce, or Tiger, Hog, or bearded Goat,
> All other parts remaining as they were.
> *(ll. 70–73)*

This "foul disfigurement" recalls Rachel's dream after Dalloway's kiss, of men with animal faces, an image that will return
in her delirium.

The description of Rachel's illness is the finest sustained writing in the novel. It is a compelling rendering of a psychotic state:
the inward preoccupation, the disconnectedness from ordinary
concerns, the way in which simple actions, like a nurse playing cards, may appear sinister. Woolf finds language to convey
the perceptual changes—the fluidity and instability of the visual
world, walls that appear curved, the floor that seems unstable,

trees seen through a window that appear too near or too far off:

> Helen sometimes said that it was lunchtime, and
> sometimes that it was teatime; but by the next day
> all landmarks were obliterated, and the outer world
> was so far away that the different sounds such as the
> sounds of people moving overhead could only be as-
> cribed to their cause by a great effort of memory.
> The recollection of what she had felt, or of what she
> had been doing and thinking three days before, had
> faded entirely. On the other hand, every object in
> the room, and the bed itself, and her own body with
> its various limbs and their different sensations were
> more and more important each day. She was com-
> pletely cut off, and unable to communicate with the
> rest of the world, isolated alone with her body. (312)

Time becomes distorted through the long hours of sleepless nights: "Having turned on her pillow Rachel woke to find herself in the midst of one of those interminable nights which do not end at twelve, but go on into the double figures—thirteen, fourteen, and so on until they reach the twenties, and then the thirties, and then the forties. She realized that there is nothing to prevent nights from doing this if they choose" (312). In the course of her illness Rachel has a hallucination that is a reprise of her dream after Dalloway's kiss, but now the tunnel, with its oozing damp walls, contains not men but little deformed old women who eventually become Helen and Nurse McInnis. When Terence, sitting by her bedside, kisses her, she opens her eyes but sees only an old woman slicing off a man's head with a knife. Her hallucination recalls the scene of horrifying, casual violence by the women in the courtyard.

Finally the end approaches, described in language that encompasses at once both the approaching death and the psychotic fantasies of the fictional Rachel—and prefigures Woolf's own suicide:

> For six days indeed she had been oblivious of the world outside, because it needed all her attention to follow the hot, red, quick sights which passed incessantly before her eyes. She knew that it was of enormous importance that she should attend to these sights and grasp their meaning, but she was always being just too late to hear or see something which would explain it all. For this reason, the faces,— Helen's face, the nurse's, Terence's, the doctor's,— which occasionally forced themselves very close to her, were worrying because they distracted her attention and she might miss the clue. . . . At last the faces went further away; she fell into a deep pool of sticky water, which eventually closed over her head. She saw nothing and heard nothing but a faint booming sound, which was the sea rolling over her head. While all her tormentors thought that she was dead, she was not dead, but curled up at the bottom of the sea. (322)

Terence tries to find comfort by imagining a reality beyond that which we see: "Surely the world of strife and fret and anxiety was not the real world, but this was the real world, the world that lay beneath the superficial world, so that, whatever happened, one was secure." But as Terence realizes, through the nurse's evasions, that he will in fact lose Rachel, his comforting thought turns into its opposite. He sees that what lies beyond the world of appearances is more sinister still: "He had never realised before that underneath every action, underneath the life of every day, pain lies, quiescent, but ready to devour; he seemed to be able to see suffering, as if it were a fire, curling up over the edges of all action, eating away the lives of men and women. . . . Never again would he feel secure; he would never believe in the stability of life, or forget what depths of pain lie beneath small happiness and feelings of content and safety" (325).

Terence's changing sense of what lies beyond the world of appearances recalls a passage in an earlier version of the novel, an interior monologue of Rachel. The starting point for her reflections is a volume of Cowper's letters. In the published novel, Rachel tosses the book aside as boring. In the earlier version, however, far from tossing Cowper aside, Rachel finds in him a kindred spirit: "That he would go mad again was evident; the deeps of melancholy were all about him." And then Rachel's thoughts continue,

> "They are real, these dead people," was her conclusion. She put her hand up, and fancied she felt the faint shock of the things he had thought a century ago, tingling, like wireless messages upon the palm. . . . "Come, Spirits," she murmured; and was instantly fortified by a sense of the presence of the things that aren't there. There were the beautiful drowned statues, there were the glens and hills of an undiscovered country; there were divine musical notes, which, struck high up in the air, made ones heart beat with delight at the assurance that the world of things that aren't there was splendidly alive and far more real than the other.

The world of "things that aren't there" is the world of imagination and art; it is also the world of the dead. In this passage in an early, unpublished version of the novel, the dead are fortifying presences, splendidly alive; at other times these "invisible presences," as Woolf would later call them, haunted and tormented her.

In an early draft of *The Voyage Out* there is an exchange between Rachel and Terence as she is telling him about her life in Richmond with her aunts: "Then she stopped. He could see that she was struggling whether to tell him or not, and she could not speak lest she should burst into tears. A picture had come before her eyes, which she could not pass directly, a picture of her mother stooping over her and saying good night."

It is clear what is meant by the odd use of the word "pass": Rachel is trying to pass over or dismiss the memory, but the picture insistently presses itself upon her. Terence asks if she remembers her mother, and she nods. At this point she "longed that he take her in his arms but made up her mind to go on, pass it, and succeeded. She could not ask him to take her in his arms as she wanted to." This is the only instance in any version of this novel, published or unpublished, of physical longing of a woman toward a man. Significantly, her longing is for him to comfort her, to substitute for the physical presence of the mother she had lost. And we hear, now, that the name of the man, Terence, is very like the name of Rachel's mother, Teresa—the name that is hardly spoken in the novel.

The picture that comes before Rachel's eyes is a child's memory, of herself small and her mother stooping over her. It anticipates an extraordinary scene that is present, with variations, in each of the surviving early manuscripts but that disappears from the published version of the novel. Disappears—but not without a trace. It survives as a strange and disturbing passage, what Heine (1990, 425) calls "one of the most powerful and puzzling moments in the novel." Having declared their love for each other and begun to speak of marriage, Rachel and Terence attempt to find their way back from their walk in the woods. As they try to rejoin the others,

> voices crying behind them never reached through the waters in which they were now sunk. The repetition of Hewet's name in short, dissevered syllables was to them the crack of a dry branch or the laughter of a bird. The grasses and breezes sounding and murmuring all round them, they never noticed that the swishing of the grasses grew louder and louder, and did not cease with the lapse of the breeze. A hand dropped abrupt as iron on Rachel's shoulder; it might have been a bolt from heaven. She fell beneath it, and the grass whipped across her eyes and filled her mouth and ears. Through the waving stems she saw a figure, large and shapeless against the sky. Helen was upon her. Rolled this way and that, now seeing only forests of green, and now the high blue heaven, she was speechless and almost without sense. At last she lay still, all the grasses shaken round her and before her by her panting. Over her loomed two great heads, the heads of a man and woman, of Terence and Helen.
>
> Both were flushed, both laughing, and lips were moving; they came together and kissed in the air above her. Broken fragments of speech came down to her on the ground. (268)

In the published version, the passage is dreamlike and difficult to follow.

But the earlier versions of this scene in the unpublished manuscripts are altogether lucid. There is no difficulty in following their content. The holograph and later typescript versions are similar; here is the passage as it appears in the holograph:

> Helen was off, sweeping through the long grass at a considerable pace. The figures continuing to retreat, she broke into a run, uttering Rachel's name in breathless gasps/shouts. Rachel heard at last; looked round, saw the figure of her Aunt only a hundred yards away and at once took to her heels. Terence stopped. But Helen swept past him, cantering over the waving ground like one of the deer themselves, pulling handfuls of grass and casting them at Rachel's back, abusing her roundly as she did so. Here Rachel was at fault. She turned to look, caught her foot in a twist of grass and fell headlong. Helen was upon her. Too breathless to scold she spent her rage in rolling the helpless body hither and thither, holding both wrists in one firm grasp, and stuffing eyes ears nose and mouth with the feathery seeds of the grass.
>
> Finally she laid her flat on the ground, her arms out on either side of her, her hat off, her hair down.
>
> "Own yourself beaten!" she gasped. "And beg my pardon!" Lying thus flat, Rachel saw Helen's head pendent above her, very large against the sky. A second head loomed above it. "Help! Terence!" she cried.
>
> "I've a right to protect her," he exclaimed, when Helen was for protesting. "We're going to be married." For the next few seconds they rolled indiscriminately in a bundle, imparting handsful of grass together with attempted kisses. Separating at last,

and attempting to tidy her hair, Helen exclaimed, "Yesterday! I knew it!"

It is a passage of fierce eroticism between two women. "Breathless," "panting," "gasping," "hat off," "hair down"—the scene is one of nearly explicit sexuality. Indeed, in the earlier typescript, instead of fleeing Rachel opens her arms to the older woman, welcoming her advance; the verbs that describe their speech to one another, "murmuring," "whispering," "breathing," leave no doubt about their physical intimacy.

The pursuing Helen is rageful, possessive, forcing Rachel down when she tries to get up, holding both of her wrists, rolling her helpless body back and forth. Helen's stuffing Rachel's eyes, ears, nose, and mouth with seeds suggests a fantasy of rape by another woman. In this fantasy, the older woman is an irresistible, terrifying force, powerful and potentially murderous: in a typescript version of the scene, Helen knocks Rachel down when she tries to get up and keeps one hand upon her throat, holding her head down among the grasses. And in a still earlier version, Helen not only demands that Rachel beg her pardon, presumably for marrying Terence, but goes further: "Beg my pardon, and say that you worship me!" Trying to flee from Helen, Rachel cries out to Terence to help her, but Helen sweeps past him. The man is merely a bystander, all but irrelevant. His attempt to protect Rachel seems wan and foolish, no match for Helen's force.

In the holograph version of the scene, on the page facing the text, there is a sketch, presumably done by Woolf herself. It is upside down, and it takes up an entire page. It is a charcoal sketch of a woman. As much as the published text suggests a fear of male sexuality and of marriage, the earlier manuscripts suggest a powerful erotic pull toward women, specifically toward an older woman who is a maternal figure, and a fear of her imagined power. The manuscript versions of this scene are indeed "unguarded," as Woolf declared first novels are apt to be. They suggest what she was struggling both to say and to silence, and why, therefore, the version she chose to publish is so difficult to read.

There is a passage in a very early draft that disappears entirely in the published novel. It is about Rachel's mother, and it is richly evocative. She was

> a great voluptuous woman, the daughter of a parson in the north country, had wished of course to breed sons, whom she figured as bold defenders and besiegers, rough stalwart men, who were to express for her by their excessive vigour and scorn of femininity her own spite against the restrictions of her sex. . . . Still Mrs Vinrace was too generous a nature to stint her affections voluntarily; and in time she had as passionate a feeling for her daughter, but it was more jealous, more easily on the defensive, than any that she might have had for her sons. But she died; and left as legacy to her child a number of speculations which as her mother would never answer them, might be considered with the utmost candour from very different points of view. Her mother for instance, would put into action her own most hidden impulses; pulling down a branch weighted with apple blossom and shaking it so that the petals dropped in a long chain to the ground and the whole burden of autumn fruit vanished in a moment. Such traits in her mother she loved and feared. (*Melymbrosia*, 264)

At first glance it is a lyrical picture — branches of apple blossoms and petals and autumn fruit — but the first glance is deceptive. In fact the mother's act is destructive, killing life in its most tender and vulnerable state.

The enactment of the mother's "most hidden impulses" may be understood as the primitive fantasies or projections of a young child. Because her mother had died when she was young, Rachel was left with what are called in the manuscript "a number of speculations"—wonderings, imaginings, projections, longings, terrors, fantasies—which could not be measured against or tempered by the day-to-day realities of life. The mother who died remains, for Rachel Vinrace and for Virginia Woolf, both passionately loved and passionately feared. It is the mother who haunts Virginia Woolf's first "work of the imagination." As Rachel astutely asks, "Or do people die?"

8

"On Being Ill"

In 1925, unable to begin work on the autobiographical novel she had envisaged because she was ill for a period of months, Virginia Woolf produced an essay on illness itself. It appeared in January 1926 in T. S. Eliot's *New Criterion*. Ostensibly about the ordinary illnesses that everyone experiences at some time or other, the "daily drama of the body"—fever, toothache, flu—the essay "On Being Ill" moves beyond these commonplace ailments, familiar to all, to encompass tacitly the experience of psychosis and to reflect upon the relation between body and mind. The essay offers a point of entry into the subject of Woolf's own complex response to the illness that haunted her for much of her life, manic-depressive illness.

The essay begins with a shimmering and engaging—and extremely long—opening sentence:

> Considering how common illness is, how tremendous the spiritual change that it brings, how astonishing, when the lights of health go down, the undiscovered countries that are then disclosed, what wastes and deserts of the soul a slight attack of influenza brings to light, what precipices and lawns sprinkled with bright flowers a little rise of temperature reveals, what ancient and obdurate oaks are uprooted in us in the act of sickness, how we go down into the pit of death and feel the waters of annihilation close above our heads and wake thinking to find ourselves in the presence of the angels and the

harpers when we have a tooth out and come to the
surface in the dentist's arm chair and confuse his
'Rinse the mouth—rinse the mouth' with the greet-
ing of the Deity stooping from the floor of Heaven
to welcome us—when we think of this and infinitely
more, as we are so frequently forced to think of it,
it becomes strange indeed that illness has not taken
its place with love, battle, and jealousy among the
prime themes of literature. (*Essays* 4:317)

The sentence has the cadence of a peroration: the author wants
to *persuade* us. At the outset there is a crescendo in the weight
and intensity of her adjectives—how "common," how "tremendous," how "astonishing"—and then she suddenly turns and
mocks the grandeur of her rhetoric. What seems to be the greet-
ing of the Deity stooping from the floor of Heaven is really
the dentist saying, "Rinse the mouth—rinse the mouth." But
Woolf's point is that the seemingly disparate realms of body and
soul are in fact inseparable. The body is not a sheet of plain glass
through which the soul looks straight and clear: the state of the
body affects what is "seen." The whole notion of how we "see"
will be questioned here, with the implication that the verb does
indeed deserve to be placed in quotation marks. The metaphor
that flashes by in this tumble of clauses in the long opening sentence begins to suggest—mischievously, subversively, contrary
to common sense—that it is light that conceals and darkness
that reveals.

But of all this, Woolf argues, there is no record in literature. Compared with the themes of love and battle and jealousy,
"those great wars which the body wages with the mind a slave
to it, in the solitude of the bedroom against the assault of fever
or the oncome of melancholia, are neglected." The glancing reference to melancholia here is the only explicit acknowledgment

that the illness she is speaking of encompasses mental as well as physical illness: indeed, the thrust of her argument is to eradicate the distinction between the physical and the mental, between body and mind. One hindrance to the description of illness in literature is the poverty of language: "English, which can express the thoughts of Hamlet and the tragedy of Lear, has no words for the shiver and the headache. . . . The merest schoolgirl, when she falls in love, has Shakespeare, Donne, Keats to speak her mind for her; but let a sufferer try to describe a pain in his head to a doctor and language at once runs dry."

Though Woolf grounds her argument in such commonplace ailments as a pain in the head, the pangs of sciatica, and the flu, her description may also be read as a succinct description of psychosis: the perceptual changes, the sense of being at a distance from ordinary human concerns, the transformation in the appearance of other people, extreme alterations in the sense of self:

> "I am in bed with influenza"—but what does that convey of the great experience; how the world has changed its shape; the tools of business grown remote; the sounds of festival become romantic like a merry-go-round heard across far fields; and friends have changed, some putting on a strange beauty, others deformed to the squatness of toads, while the whole landscape of life lies remote and fair, like the shore seen from a ship far out at sea, and he is now on a peak and needs no help from man or God, and now grovels supine on the floor glad of a kick from a housemaid—the experience cannot be imparted. (*Essays* 4:319)

The description she crafts is compelling in its particularity, even as she insists that the experience cannot be imparted in words.

We need a new language, she argues, one that is "primitive, subtle, sensual, obscene."

While Woolf protests the poverty of language for describing it, one of the claims she makes for illness is its power to enhance the experience of language, for as the meanings of words recede, their sensory qualities are heightened. Words become sound, and scent, and taste: "In illness words seem to possess a mystic quality . . . In health meaning has encroached upon sound. Our intelligence domineers over our senses. But in illness, with the police off duty, we creep beneath some obscure poem by Mallarmé or Donne, some phrase in Latin or Greek, and the words give out their scent, and ripple like leaves, and chequer us with light and shadow, and then, if at last we grasp the meaning, it is all the richer for having travelled slowly up with all the bloom upon its wings" (*Essays* 4:324).

In illness an adult can recapture a young child's experience of language, when the sensory qualities of words are more vivid than they will be once meaning asserts itself and, as Woolf says, "domineers." And in illness there is a childish outspokenness; truths are blurted out which the cautious respectability of health conceals. In health, a "genial pretence must be kept up"; in illness that make-believe ceases. And the essential truth that is revealed in this state, starkly, is the aloneness of each individual: "That illusion of a world so shaped that it echoes every groan, of human beings so tied together by common needs and fears that a twitch at one wrist jerks another, where however strange your experience other people have had it too, where however far you travel in your own mind someone has been there before you — is all an illusion. We do not know our own souls, let alone the souls of others. Human beings do not go hand in hand the whole stretch of the way" (*Essays* 4:320).

In illness, "we cease to be soldiers in the army of the upright; we become deserters. They march to battle. We float with the sticks on the stream; helter skelter with the dead leaves on the lawn, irresponsible and disinterested and able, perhaps for the first time for years, to look round, to look up—to look, for example, at the sky." Not only human relationships, but nature itself is seen more fully, more honestly: "It is only the recumbent who know what, after all, Nature is at no pains to conceal—that she in the end will conquer; heat will leave the world; stiff with frost we shall cease to drag ourselves about the fields; ice will lie thick upon factory and engine; the sun will go out." Illness strips away the pretenses that civilization requires. "It is only the recumbent who know," she asserts, returning to the reversals of her opening paragraph: it is light that conceals and darkness that reveals.

Ostensibly, as I said, Woolf's essay is about the common aches and pains that all flesh is heir to: but the larger claims that she makes point to her experience of psychosis and depression. Although doctors gave contradictory assessments and advice, Woolf herself was convinced that what she had was an illness, a vulnerability to which, she intuited, was hereditary. As she put it, "My nervous system being a second hand one, used by my father and his father to dictate dispatches and write books with—how I wish they had hunted and fished instead!—I have to treat it like a pampered pug dog, and lie still directly my head aches" (*Letters* 4:145). And again, "I am, like my father, 'skinless': oversensitive and nervously irritable" (*Letters* 5:408). From the vantage point of the present, it is clear that Virginia Woolf suffered from manic-depressive illness.[1] Moreover, she was cor-

---

1. The diagnosis of "bipolar disorder" was introduced in the DSM-IV (*Diagnostic and Statistical Manual,* 1994), but I have favored the earlier, more descriptive term. Jamison (1993) discusses the incidence of manic-depressive illness in poets, writers, and artists in the light of a contemporary understanding of this illness, and in her memoir (1995) gives a

rect in her intuition that this illness has a hereditary component. In her time, however, psychiatry had little to offer her in the way of treatment beyond the recommendation that she rest.

In his autobiography, Leonard Woolf looks back over the years of his marriage to Virginia and conveys, in the rhythms of their life, the frequent hover of the *possibility* of illness: the headache that was a warning sign, the excitement, the difficulty in sleeping. When these symptoms became intense, "it might be several weeks before she could begin again to live a normal life. But four times in her life the symptoms would not go and she passed across the border which divides what we call insanity from sanity." The breakdown that began in the first year of their marriage in 1912 was the most severe she had had to that point: although the manscript of *The Voyage Out* was accepted by Duckworth & Co. in March 1913, its publication had to be delayed for two years. Leonard Woolf's description of her symptoms leaves no doubt as to the diagnosis:

> In the first stage of the illness from 1914 practically every symptom was the exact opposite of those in the second stage in 1915. In the first stage she was in the depths of depression, would hardly eat or talk, was suicidal. In the second she was in a state of violent excitement and wild euphoria, talking incessantly for long periods of time. In the first stage she was violently opposed to the nurses and they had the greatest difficulty in getting her to do anything; she wanted me to be with her continually and for a week or two I was the only person able to get her to eat anything. In the second stage of violent excitement,

compelling description of the subjective experience. See also Andreasen (1987), Andreasen and Glick (1988), and Caramagno (1992).

she was violently hostile to me, would not talk to me
or allow me to come into her room. She was occasionally violent with the nurses, but she tolerated
them in a way which was the opposite of her behavior to them in the first stage. (*Beginning Again*,
161)

In summarizing her history, he emphasizes the distinctness of
the two states:

In the manic stage she was extremely excited; the
mind raced; she talked volubly and, at the height
of the attack, incoherently; she had delusions and
heard voices, for instance she told me that in her second attack she heard the birds in the garden outside
her window talking Greek . . . During the depressive
stage all her thoughts and emotions were the exact
opposite of what they had been in the manic stage.
She was in the depths of melancholia and despair;
she scarcely spoke; refused to eat; refused to believe
that she was ill. (*Beginning Again*, 76–77)

The Woolfs consulted many doctors over the years. The futility
of their suggestions—and Leonard Woolf's own bitterness—
is epitomized by one of the Harley Street specialists they consulted, a Dr. Saintsbury, who advised the patient, "Equanimity
—equanimity—practice equanimity, Mrs. Woolf" (*Downhill
All the Way*, 51).

In the essay "On Being Ill" Woolf argued that illness should
take its place alongside the great themes of love, and war, and
jealousy as a subject for literature. She herself did write about
illness—in diaries and letters, and in the novel *Mrs. Dalloway*.
In the character of Septimus Warren Smith, Woolf gives a sus-

tained, unflinching picture of the experience of madness. It is harrowing: terror, loneliness, paranoia, grandiosity, hallucination, and ultimately suicide. The claims she made in her essay for the enhancing powers of illness disappear. Woolf also gives, in this novel, a sustained and empathic picture of the experience of the spouse of a person who is ill—perplexed, angry, despairing, alone.

Septimus Warren Smith first appears in the novel as a motor-car is making its way through the streets of London—a motor-car containing royalty, many bystanders think. As the car turns toward Buckingham Palace, people in the street speculate excitedly about who might be inside. But Septimus's eyes "had a look of apprehension in them. The world has raised its whip; where will it descend?" An airplane flies overhead, forming letters in the sky, and people are trying to make out the shapes of the letters; Septimus believes that the skywriting is signaling a message to him. Birds sing to him in Greek, as they did to Virginia Woolf during her breakdown after the death of her father.

Vividly Woolf describes her character's inner state, a state that, as she says in "On Being Ill," is nearly impossible to convey in words: "He lay very high, on the back of the world. The earth thrilled beneath him. Red flowers grew through his flesh; their stiff leaves rustled by his head. Music began clanging against the rocks up here. It is a motor horn down in the street, he muttered; but up here it cannoned from rock to rock, divided, met in shocks of sound which rose in smooth columns (that music should be visible was a discovery) and became an anthem" (*Mrs. Dalloway*, 103). A passing dog threatens to turn into a man: it is horrible, he thinks, terrible to see a dog become a man.

Woolf is describing, in the character of Septimus Smith, hallucinations and paranoid delusions, emotional lability and grandiosity. These terms are abstractions; her description has the force of particularity. Sometimes the point of view is Septimus's own, sometimes it shifts to that of his bewildered wife. He sees an old woman's head in the middle of a fern. He

> saw faces laughing at him, calling him horrible dis-
> gusting names, from the walls, and hands pointing
> round the screen. Yet they were quite alone. But
> he began to talk aloud, answering people, arguing,
> laughing, crying, getting very excited and making
> her write things down. . . . He knew all their
> thoughts, he said; he knew everything. He knew the
> meaning of the world, he said . . . he, Septimus, was
> alone, called forth in advance of the mass of men to
> hear the truth, to learn the meaning, which now at
> last, after all the toils of civilisation—Greeks, Ro-
> mans, Shakespeare, Darwin, and now himself—was
> to be given whole to . . . "To whom?" he asked aloud.
> "To the Prime Minister," the voices which rustled
> about his head replied. (101-02)

Septimus exists in a solipsistic world in which the impinge-
ments of reality—a Skye terrier passing, his wife's voice—become materials to be transformed through his preoccupations
and delusions. When his wife returns with flowers, saying as she
arranges them that she had had to buy them from a poor man
in the street and that they were almost dead already, Septimus's
fevered imagination transmutes these elements: "So there was
a man outside; Evans presumably; and the roses, which Rezia
said were half dead, had been picked by him in the fields of
Greece" (141).

Here, then, is the heart of the matter. Septimus's friend,
Evans, had been killed in the war, just before the Armistice.
The two men had been inseparable, but when he learned of his

friend's death "Septimus, far from showing any emotion or rec-
ognising that here was the end of a friendship, congratulated
himself upon feeling very little and very reasonably" (130). An
earlier version of the novel had quoted repeatedly, as a refrain, a
phrase from Shelley's *Adonais:* "Can never mourn."

The difficulty with not mourning the death of his friend,
though Septimus congratulated himself upon his own reasonableness, is that the state of feeling very little cannot remain
circumscribed. After the truce was signed and the dead buried,
Septimus had "sudden thunder-claps of fear. He could not feel."
In Milan, he was billeted in the house of an innkeeper with two
daughters who made hats, and "one evening when the panic was
on him—that he could not feel" he became engaged to one of
the daughters. Septimus chose the gay younger daughter, as if
her cheerful pleasure in the ordinary could save him from despair, as if her rootedness in the concrete details of life—the
feathers, spangles, silks, and ribbons of the milliner's trade—
could hold him to that reality: "Scissors rapping, girls laughing, hats being made protected him; he was assured of safety;
he had a refuge. But he could not sit there all night. There were
moments of waking in the early morning. The bed was falling;
he was falling. Oh for the scissors and the lamplight and the
buckram shapes!" (131).

Septimus's sense of defect in himself is projected onto the external world: when the "appalling fear" came over him that he
could not feel, Septimus decided that "his brain was perfect; it
must be the fault of the world then—that he could not feel."
This is the starting point for the psychotic state: the perceptual alterations, delusions, hallucinations, and the compensa-
tory feeling of grandiose self-sufficiency. And as vividly as Woolf
conveys the psychotic state of Septimus, she conveys the tenderness and bewilderment and anger of the young wife, Lucrezia,
alone with her husband in a strange country: "It was not mar-

riage; it was not being one's husband to look strange like that, always to be starting, laughing, sitting hour after hour silent, or clutching her and telling her to write ... And he was always stopping in the middle, changing his mind; wanting to add something; hearing something new; listening with his hand up. But she heard nothing" (212–13).

In her naiveté Lucrezia hopes that doctors can help. Dr. Holmes and then Sir William Bradshaw are scathingly portrayed by Woolf. They are full of irrelevant pomposity, knowing nothing at all about the condition they are called upon to treat. Both are worldly men, Dr. Holmes having an eye for the pretty young Italian wife. He displays a genial, self-congratulatory ignorance of Septimus's state: "When he felt like that he went to the Music Hall, said Dr. Holmes. He took a day off with his wife and played golf. Why not try two tabloids of bromide dissolved in a glass of water at bedtime?" (137). He brushes aside the "headaches, sleeplessness, fears, dreams" (Woolf's own familiar symptoms) as "nerve symptoms and nothing more." Health, he declares, "is largely a matter in our own control. Throw yourself into outside interests; take up some hobby."

The second expert, Sir William Bradshaw, unlike Dr. Holmes, recognizes the seriousness of the case but is no more useful. He cuts a more powerful figure than the bumbling Dr. Holmes, and the portrait of him is more bitter: "Worshipping proportion, Sir William not only prospered himself but made England prosper, secluded her lunatics, forbade childbirth, penalised despair, made it impossible for the unfit to propagate their views until they, too, shared his sense of proportion—his, if they were men, Lady Bradshaw's if they were women." Pompous and self-satisfied, Sir William has a theory: "You invoke proportion; order rest in bed; rest in solitude; silence and rest; rest without friends, without books, without messages; six months' rest" (150). It is a devastating portrayal: in the end Sir William's thoroughgoing ignorance and self-certainty contribute to Septimus's suicide as much as the inner demons that torment him.

When Virginia Woolf was acutely ill, she did not write. Thus the diaries and letters that so richly document her life do not, on the whole, document the experience of psychosis in the present tense. There is one exception, a period of weeks during which she did attempt to record the experience as it was happening. Between the end of July and the beginning of September 1926, Woolf narrated in her diary "a whole nervous breakdown in miniature." In early June of that year she had had a "nerve exhaustion headache," whose effect she described in a letter:

> One's back seems to be made of a membrane, like
> a bats wing: this should be stretched tight, in order
> to deal adequately with the flight of existence; but
> suddenly it flops, and becomes (I imagine) like a veil
> (do you remember the veils of our youth?) which has
> fallen into a cup of tea. So I am lying on the sofa, in
> my nightgown, picking at a book or two, and drop-
> ping them on to the floor. I see nobody partly be-
> cause I have nothing to say except oh! Shall I ever
> have anything to say except oh! (*Letters* 3:272)

On the last day of June 1926, she had noted in her diary that she was in black despair because Clive Bell had laughed at her new hat: she was "as unhappy as I have been these ten years; & revolved it in sleep & dreams all night; & today has been ruined" (*Diary* 3:91). She was well aware of the disproportion between the cause and the magnitude of its emotional effect: "I bring home minute pinpricks which magnify in the middle of the night into gaping wounds."

She had set aside work on *To the Lighthouse* until she and Leonard would return to Rodmell at the end of July: "There I shall come to grips with the last part of that python, my book; it is a tug & a struggle, & I wonder now & then, why I let myself in for it" (96). This is hardly the blowing of "bubbles through a pipe" she would recall in her memoir, in which she looked back on the composition of *To the Lighthouse* as though it had been effortless, coming to her in a "great, apparently involuntary rush," her lips "syllabling of their own accord." It is beguiling description, but diaries and letters over the period when she was composing the novel complicate the picture. She had been planning to begin work on it in the summer of 1925. The diary entry that I quoted in chapter 1, in which Woolf describes the book as she envisaged it ("This is going to be fairly short: to have father's character done complete in it; & mothers. . . .") is dated May 14, 1925—the day that *Mrs. Dalloway* was published. As always, Woolf began one book as she finished the last, so that there would be no time when she was not writing. This entry continues, "I must write a few little stories first, & let the Lighthouse simmer, adding to it between tea & dinner till it is complete for writing out."

"Can hardly bear to keep my fingers off a new novel," she wrote to Vita Sackville-West on May 27, "but swear I won't start til August." In fact, however, on August 19 at a birthday party for her nephew she fainted, and was bedridden on and off until December, living "that odd amphibious life of headache." She was able to begin work on *To the Lighthouse* in January, but her writing was interrupted again in the summer. This time she undertook to make a record of the breakdown. It is a richly interesting document in which she describes in detail the subjective experience, day by day, and reflects upon its relation to her art.

In form, it is a series of notes in her diary. In the first of these she says about her own thoughts, "Suppose one could catch them before they became 'works of art'? Catch them hot & sudden as they rise in the mind. . . . Of course one cannot; for the process of language is slow & deluding." And there follows a passage she titled "My own Brain":

> Here is a whole nervous breakdown in miniature. We came [to Rodmell] on Tuesday. Sank into a chair, could scarcely rise; everything insipid; taste-less, colourless. Enormous desire for rest. Wednes-day—only wish to be alone in the open air. Air de-licious—avoided speech; could not read. Thought of my own power of writing with veneration, as of something incredible, belonging to someone else; never again to be enjoyed by me. Mind a blank. Slept in my chair. Thursday. No pleasure in life whatsoever; but felt perhaps more attuned to exis-tence. Character and idiosyncracy as Virginia Woolf completely sunk out. Humble & modest. Difficulty in thinking what to say. Read automatically, like a cow chewing cud. Slept in chair. Friday. Sense of physical tiredness; but slight activity of the brain. Beginning to take notice. . . . Saturday (today) much clearer & lighter. Thought I could write, but re-sisted, or found it impossible. A desire to read poetry set in on Friday. This brings back a sense of my own individuality. Read some Dante & Bridges, with-out troubling to understand, but got pleasure from them. Now I begin to wish to write notes, but not yet novel. But today senses quickening. No "making up" power yet; no desire to cast scenes in my book. (*Diary* 3:103)

In another entry she describes the perceptual changes she ex-perienced: how the proportions of the landscape were suddenly altered and people in a meadow appear to be sunk far down on a flat board. Detail is smoothed out; the colours of the women's dresses appear very bright and pure. The proportions are "abnormal," she says, and at the same time they seem to her extremely beautiful.

In an entry she called "Returning Health" Woolf traces the gradual return of her ability to write: "This is shown by the power to make images: the suggestive power of every sight & word is enormously increased. Shakespeare must have had this to an extent which makes my normal state the state of a person blind, deaf, dumb, stone-stockish & fish-blooded. And I have it compared with poor Mrs Bartholomew [their sometime cook] almost to the extent that Sh[akespea]re has it compared with me" (*Diary* 3:104). This altered state in which the visual world is transformed, in which the sensory properties of language are heightened to an extraordinary degree, she regards as the mark of genius: it is a gift that is bestowed, in differing degrees, or denied entirely. That is one view Virginia Woolf held. And here is another, from an entry two weeks later:

> Oh its beginning its coming—the horror—physically like a painful wave swelling about the heart —tossing me up. I'm unhappy unhappy! Down— God, I wish I were dead . . . I've only a few years to live I hope. I cant face this horror any more—(this is the wave spreading out over me).
>
> This goes on; several times, with varieties of horror. . . . Why have I so little control? It is not creditable, nor lovable. It is the cause of much waste & pain in my life. (*Diary* 3:110-11)

In her depressed state, she envied Vanessa "humming & booming & flourishing over the hill" nearby, referring not only to her painting but also, I think, to her happiness in motherhood. It was Woolf's lifelong sorrow not to have had children, for which she blamed, at various times, Leonard, and her doctors, and herself, as though her illness were subject to her will: "A little more self-control on my part, & we might have had a boy of 12, a girl of 10: This always rakes me wretched in the early hours." Depressed, she envied Vanessa and quarreled with Leonard: "I saw myself, my brilliancy, genius, charm, beauty (&c. &c.—the attendants who float me through so many years) diminish & disappear. One is in truth rather an elderly dowdy fussy ugly incompetent woman vain, chattering & futile" (*Diary* 3:111).

And yet, for all the anguish that she has been recording in her diary since the end of July, this entry continues, "But it is always a question whether I wish to avoid these glooms. . . . These 9 weeks give one a plunge into deep waters. . . . There is an edge to it which I feel of great importance. . . . One goes down into the well & nothing protects one from the assault of truth" (112).

The diary of the summer of 1926 documents a period when Woolf was paralyzed by depression, withdrawn from human contact, unable to work, unable even to speak, when the horror and the terror of her experience made her long for death. And yet, emerging from this state, she looks back upon it as something invaluable. Though she has been battered by the experience—her word "assaulted" has an edge of violence—she raises the question whether she would avoid these periods, even if that were possible. Painful as they are, unprotected as she feels, she finds in these periods of illness some deeper truth. It is the argument of the essay "On Being Ill."

The question she raises here is one she posed in diaries and letters over the course of a lifetime. At times she railed against her illness, felt frustrated and impeded by it, and at other times she felt that it was essential to her. She returned to the question again and again, contradicting herself without coming to a resolution. Was her illness a terrible obstacle to her art, or was it the necessary condition for it?

In a letter Woolf wrote in 1930, at the age of forty-eight, she looked back on her protracted breakdown of 1913-15, which followed both the completion of her first novel and her marriage to Leonard Woolf:

> And then I married, and then my brains went up in a shower of fireworks. As an experience, madness is terrific I can assure you, and not to be sniffed at; and in its lava I still find most of the things I write about. It shoots out of one everything shaped, final, not in mere driblets, as sanity does. And the six months . . . that I lay in bed taught me a good deal about what is called oneself. Indeed I was almost crippled when I came back to the world, unable to move a foot in terror, after that discipline. Think—not one moment's freedom from doctor discipline—perfectly strange —conventional men; 'you shant read this' and 'you shant write a word' and 'you shall lie still and drink milk'—for 6 months. (*Letters* 4:180)

Earlier that year, she had mused in her diary, "I believe these illnesses are in my case—how shall I express it?—partly mystical. Something happens in my mind. It refuses to go on registering impressions. It shuts itself up. It becomes chrysalis. . . . Then suddenly something springs . . . & this is I believe the moth shaking its wings in me. I then begin to make up my story whatever it is; ideas rush in me; often though this is before I can control my mind or pen. It is no use trying to write at this stage" (*Diary* 3:287). Similarly, while she was struggling to write *The Waves* (its working title was "The Moths"): "These curious intervals in life—I've had many—are the most fruitful artistically—one becomes fertilised—think of my madness at Hogarth—& all the little illnesses—that before I wrote To The Lighthouse for instance. Six weeks in bed now would make a masterpiece of

Moths" (*Diary* 3:254). Yet with equal conviction she could also declare the opposite: "Give me no illness for a year, 2 years, and I would write 3 novels straight off" (*Letters* 3:232).

After a two-month period in 1921 during which she was unable to work because of headaches and sleeplessness, she bemoans the time that she has lost and then continues, "Let me make a vow that this shall never, never, happen again; & *then* confess that there are some compensations. To be tired & authorised to lie in bed is pleasant; then, scribbling 365 days of the year as I do, merely to receive without agitation of my right hand in giving out is salutary. I feel that I can take stock of things in a leisurely way. Then the dark underworld has its fascinations as well as its terrors" (*Diary* 2:125–26). The dark underworld is at once fascinating and terrifying. In this passage, bedrest is welcome—pleasant and salutary. But more often she railed against the inactivity that was enforced during her illnesses, which she felt deprived her of all that was most sustaining to her. In a diary entry just ten days later, she describes an "intolerable fit of fidgets to write away":

> Here I am chained to my rock: forced to do nothing:
> doomed to let every worry, spite, irritation & obses-
> sion scratch & claw & come again. This is to say that
> I may not walk, & must not work. Whatever book
> I read bubbles up in my mind as part of an article I
> want to write. No one in the whole of Sussex is so
> miserable as I am; or so conscious of an infinite ca-
> pacity of enjoyment hoarded in me, could I use it
> . . . what wouldn't I give to be coming through Firle
> woods, dusty & hot, with my nose turned home,
> every muscle tired, & the brain laid up in sweet lav-
> ender, so sane & cool, & ripe for the morrows task.
> How I should notice everything—the phrase for it

coming the moment after & fitting like a glove; &
then on the dusty road, as I ground my pedals, so
my story would begin telling itself; & then the sun
would be down, & home, & some bout of poetry
after dinner, half read, half lived, as if the flesh were
dissolved & through it the flowers burst red &
white.

There! I've written out half my irritation. (*Diary*
2:132–33)

Here she describes the creative process as an involuntary experience of sheer pleasure. Perception is heightened, phrases suggest themselves, the story tells itself. Sometimes she felt as if the
experience were happening *to* her; at other times writing was
something she made herself do. She "writes out" irritation, she
"writes out" depression, she "writes out" horrors. Such phrases
occur again and again, in diaries and letters beginning as early
as the diary of 1897, when she was fifteen. Toward the end of
1920, looking back through her diary for that year, she reflects,
"I ought to say how happy I am, since one of these pages said
how unhappy I was. I can't see any reason in it. My only guess is
that it has something to do with working steadily; writing things
out of my head" (*Diary* 2:80).

But when she was ill or when impending illness was signaled
by a headache, the inevitable prescription meant giving up the
only effective therapy she knew: "I was almost submerged by
headache—only mine aren't headaches, but enraged rats gnawing at the nape of my neck. I went to a doctor, at length; but
all the comfort I got was that in 20 years, when I'm dead, and
dont want a head, they will be able to cure them—its a gland
that gets tired, so they say—by injections. At the moment, the
cure is too risky, so I had to fall back on old Savage's prescription—dont write or read or do anything you like doing" (*Letters*

6:76–77). It is a chillingly prescient statement: there would be no effective treatment for bipolar disorder until years after her death. During her lifetime—and here she refers back to the doctor who first treated her when she was twenty-two—what was prescribed deprived her of all that she found most sustaining.

Woolf was bitter about the time wasted when she was ill and unable to work. It was not just the periods of breakdown; it was the constant hover of the possibility of falling ill. The characteristic headache would be a signal for bedrest, the setting aside of work, and withdrawal from the social intercourse she relished. Her husband monitored her closely, and she chafed, at times, against the limits he imposed, "with the old rigid obstacle—my health." She resented living during the early years of their married life in Richmond, which he thought more calming for her, rather than in London. "Always to catch trains, always to waste time . . . I want freer intercourse, wider intercourse." When finally Leonard relented, she was jubilant: "London thou art a jewel of jewels, & jasper of jocunditie," she exclaimed in her diary (January 9, 1924). Nonetheless, looking back over the years in Richmond, she reflected, "I've had curious visions in this room, lying in bed, mad . . . I've heard the voices of the dead here. And felt, through it all, exquisitely happy."

Exquisite happiness, profound gloom, terror, longing for death—her emotional life was marked by extremes and contradictions. As she wrote to a friend, "I wish you could live in my brain for a week. It is washed with the most violent waves of emotion. What about? I dont know. It begins on waking; and I never know which—shall I be happy? Shall I be miserable" (*Letters* 3:245).

One thing she was certain of: her illness was inextricable from her writing. At work on *To the Lighthouse*, she describes herself as "keeping my imaginary people going. Not that they are people: what one imagines, in a novel, is a world. Then, when one has imagined this world, suddenly people come in—but I don't know why one does it, or why it should alleviate the misery of life, and yet not make one exactly happy; for the strain is too great" (*Letters* 3:238–39). This passage, like others I have quoted, suggests that there were times when she felt herself to be passive in the creative process. Characters, images, even language came to her unbidden. She said of *Women & Fiction* that "I used to make it up at such a rate that when I got pen & paper I was like a water bottle turned upside down. The writing was as quick as my hand could write; too quick, for now I am toiling to revise" (*Diary* 3:222). And again: "Once the mind gets hot it cant stop; I walk making up phrases; sit, contriving scenes; am in short in the thick of the greatest rapture known to me" (*Diary* 3:161).

The greatest rapture known to her—and a necessity. On holiday in France, she described how it felt to be away from paper and pen: "Mounting all the time steadily was my desire for words, till I envisaged a sheet of paper & pen & ink as something of miraculous desirability—could even relish the scratch as if it were a divine kind of relief to me—" (*Diary* 3:179).

Writing was divine relief; it was an "extraordinary exhilaration, that ardour & lust of creation" (*Diary* 3:129). And there were also many days when it was simply hard work, something that gave her little pleasure but that she made herself do. It was necessary that she keep writing in order to keep depression at bay: "Directly I am not working, or see the end in sight, then nothingness begins." It was for this reason, no doubt, that she began to plan each of her books just as she finished the one before, so that there would never be a gap in which she was not writing: "I pitched into my great lake of melancholy. Lord how deep it is! What a born melancholiac I am! The only way I keep afloat is by working. . . . Directly I stop working I feel that I am sinking down, down. And as usual, I feel that if I sink further I shall reach the truth" (*Diary* 3:235). Sinking under water:

the metaphor registers with particular force. We read it knowing that ultimately this is the way she would seek her death. It is an ambivalent metaphor, one whose emotional valence quickly reverses itself, even in the course of this brief entry. It is a metaphor that recurs with shifting valence throughout Woolf's diaries and letters: it is the "plunge into deep waters" in the diary entry quoted earlier, in which she acknowledges that it is always a question whether she would wish to avoid these glooms, even if it were possible.

Significantly, it is also the metaphor she uses to describe her method of working. She takes her writing board on her knee and then: "[I] let myself down, like a diver, very cautiously into the last sentence I wrote yesterday. Then perhaps after 20 minutes or it may be more, I shall see a light in the depths of the sea, and stealthily approach — for one's sentences are only an approximation, a net one flings over some sea pearl which may vanish; and if one brings it up it wont be anything like what it was when I saw it, under the sea" (*Letters* 4:223). To sink underwater is her metaphor for succumbing to depression — and for discovering sea pearls of truth.

Having dwelled, in this chapter, on Woolf's experience of her illness and her thoughts on its relation to her art, I do not wish to leave the impression that her life was only illness, with its extreme emotional states. Part of what makes the volumes of diaries and letters so compelling is that one discovers in them, in addition to extremes of emotion preserved in language of astonishing freshness, a capacity to savor the ordinary pleasures of life, to relish the excitement of London and the serenity of the countryside. Here is an example, her diary entry for January 7, 1920:

> We sit over the fire waiting for the post — the cream
> of the day, I think. Yet every part of the day here has

its merits—even the breakfast without toast. That
—however it begins—ends with Pippins; most
mornings the sun comes in; we finish in good temper; & I go off to the romantic chamber [her study]
over grass rough with frost & ground hard as brick.
Then Mrs Dedman comes to receive orders—to give
them, really, for she has planned our meals to suit
her days cooking before she comes. We share her
oven. The result is always savoury—stews & mashes
& deep many coloured dishes swimming in gravy
thick with carrots & onions. . . . The house is empty
by half past eleven; empty now at five o'clock; we
tend our fire, cook coffee, read, I find, luxuriously,
peacefully, at length. (*Diary* 2:3)

Surely, this is life at its very best, when its daily rhythms suf-
fice to give the deepest satisfaction and pleasure. In the face of
Virginia Woolf's illness, with its unpredictable buffetings, and
in the face of life's cruelty to her—its repeated sledgehammer
blows—her ability to savor ordinary human happiness with such
grace seems to me moving, and admirable, and still, in the end,
mysterious.

Bibliography

Abel, Elizabeth. 1989. *Virginia Woolf and the Fictions of Psychoanalysis.* Chicago: University of Chicago Press.

Andreasen, Nancy C. 1987. Creativity and mental illness: Prevalence rates in writers and their first-degree relatives. *Amer. J. Psychiatry* 144(10):1288–92.

———, and Ira Glick. 1988. Bipolar affective disorder and creativity: Implications and clinical management. *Comprehensive Psychiatry* 29(3):207–17.

Annan, Noel. 1984. *Leslie Stephen: The Godless Victorian.* New York: Random House.

Bell, Anne Olivier. 1990. "Editing Virginia Woolf's Diary." London: Bloomsbury Workshop.

Bell, Quentin. 1972. *Virginia Woolf: A Biography.* New York: Harcourt Brace Jovanovich.

Bell, Vanessa. 1974. *Notes on Virginia's Childhood: A Memoir.* Edited by Richard J. Schaubeck, Jr. New York: Frank Hallman.

———. 1993. *Selected Letters of Vanessa Bell.* Edited by Regina Marler. New York: Pantheon.

Bowlby, John. 1961. Processes of mourning. *Int. J. Psycho-Anal.* 44:317–40.

———. 1980. *Attachment and Loss.* Vol. 3. New York: Basic Books.

Caramagno, Thomas. 1992. *The Flight of the Mind: Virginia Woolf's Art and Manic-Depressive Illness.* Berkeley: University of California Press.

Caws, Mary Ann. 1986. *Reading Frames in Modern Fiction.* Princeton: Princeton University Press.

———. 1991. *Women of Bloomsbury.* London: Routledge.

Cook, Blanche Wiesen. 1979. "Women alone stir my imagination": Lesbianism and the cultural tradition. *Signs* 4:718–39.

Dahl, Christopher C. 1983. Virginia Woolf's "Moments of Being" and autobiographical tradition in the Stephen family. *Journal of Modern Literature* 10:175–96.

Dalsimer, Katherine. 1986. *Female Adolescence: Psychoanalytic Reflections on Literature.* New Haven: Yale University Press.

———. 1994. The vicissitudes of mourning: Virginia Woolf and *To the Lighthouse*. *Psychoanal. Study of the Child* 49:394–411.

De Salvo, Louise. 1979. Sorting, sequencing, and dating the drafts of Virginia Woolf's *The Voyage Out*. *Bulletin of Research in the Humanities* 82:271–93.

———. 1980. *Virginia Woolf's First Voyage: A Novel in the Making*. Totowa: Rowman and Littlefield.

———. 1983. 1897: Virginia Woolf at Fifteen. In *Virginia Woolf: A Feminist Slant*, edited by Jane Marcus, 78–108. Lincoln: University of Nebraska Press.

———. 1989. *Virginia Woolf: The Impact of Childhood Sexual Abuse on her Life and Work*, New York: Ballantine Books.

Fleishman, Avrom. 1975. *Virginia Woolf: A Critical Reading*. Baltimore: Johns Hopkins University Press.

Freud, S. 1899. Screen Memories. *SE 3*, 301–22.

———. 1917. Mourning and melancholia. *SE 14*, 237–60.

———. 1929. Letter to Ludwig Binswanger, April 12, 1929. In *The Letters of Sigmund Freud*, edited by E. Freud, 386. New York: Basic Books, 1960.

Furman, Erna. 1974. *A Child's Parent Dies: Studies in Childhood Bereavement*. New Haven: Yale University Press.

Furman, Robert A. 1968. Additional remarks on mourning and the young child. *Bull. Phila. Assn. for Psychoanal.* 18:51–64.

Goodwin, F. K., and Kay R. Jamison. 1990. *Manic-Depressive Illness*. New York: Oxford University Press.

Gordon, Lyndall. 1984. *Virginia Woolf: A Writer's Life*. New York: Norton.

Hamilton, James W. 1969. Object loss, dreaming, and creativity: The poetry of John Keats. *Psychoanal. Study of the Child* 14:488–531.

Heine, Elizabeth. 1990. "Virginia Woolf's Revisions of *The Voyage Out*." In *The Voyage Out*, edited by E. Heine, 399–452. London: Hogarth.

Hill, Katherine C. 1981. Virginia Woolf and Leslie Stephen: History and literary revolution. *PMLA* 96:351–62.

Hyman, Virginia. 1983. The autobiographical present in *A Sketch of the Past*. *Psychoanalytic Review* 70:24–32.

Jacobson, Edith. 1965. The return of the lost parent. In *Drives, Affects, and Behavior*, edited by M. Schur, 2:193–211. New York: International University Press.

Jamison, Kay Redfield. 1989. Mood disorders and patterns of creativity in British writers and artists. *Psychiatry* 52(2):125–34.

———. 1993. *Touched with Fire: Manic-Depressive Illness and the Artistic Temperament.* New York: Free Press.

———. 1995. *An Unquiet Mind.* New York: Knopf.

———, Robert H. Gerner, Constance Hammen, and Christine Padensky. 1980. Clouds and silver linings: Positive experiences associated with primary affective disorders. *Amer. J. Psychiatry* 137(2):198-202.

Leaska, Mitchell. 1973. Virginia Woolf's *Voyage Out:* Character deduction and the function of ambiguity. *Virginia Woolf Quarterly* 1:18-41.

———. 1977. *The Novels of Virginia Woolf from Beginning to End.* New York: John Jay Press.

Lee, Hermione. 1977. *The Novels of Virginia Woolf.* New York: Holmes and Maier.

———. 1996. *Virginia Woolf.* New York: Knopf.

Liebert, Robert S. 1983. *Michelangelo: A Psychoanalytic Study of His Life and Images.* New Haven: Yale University Press.

Loewald, Hans W. 1962. Internalization, separation, mourning, and the superego. In *Papers on Psychoanalysis,* by H. W. Loewald, 257-76. New Haven: Yale University Press, .

Love, Jean O. 1978. *Virginia Woolf: Sources of Madness and Art.* Berkeley: University of California Press.

Majumdar, R., and A. McLaurin, eds. 1975. *Virginia Woolf: The Critical Heritage.* London: Routledge.

McDowell, Frederick P. W. 1980. "Surely order did prevail": Virginia Woolf and *The Voyage Out.* In *Virginia Woolf: Revaluation and Continuity,* edited by Ralph Freedman, 73-96. Berkeley: University of California Press.

Moore, Madeline. 1981. Some female versions of pastoral: *The Voyage Out* and matriarchal mythologies. In *New Feminist Essays on Virginia Woolf,* edited by Jane Marcus, 82-104. London: Macmillan.

———. 1984. *The Short Season Between Two Silences.* Boston: George Allen and Unwin.

Pollack, George. 1961. Mourning and adaptation. *Int. J. Psycho-Anal.* 42:341-61.

———. 1989. *The Mourning-Liberation Process.* 2 vols. New York: International University Press.

Rose, Phyllis. 1978. *Woman of Letters: A Life of Virginia Woolf.* New York: Harcourt Brace Jovanovich.

Schlack, Beverly Ann. 1979. *Continuing Presences: Virginia Woolf's Use of Literary Allusion.* University Park: Pennsylvania State University Press.

Showalter, Elaine. 1985. *The Female Malady: Women, Madness, and English Culture, 1830-1980*. New York: Pantheon.

Siggins, Lorraine D. 1966. Mourning: A critical survey of the literature. *Int. J. Psycho-Anal* 47:14-25.

Spalding, Frances. 1983. *Vanessa Bell*. London: George Weidenfeld and Nicolson.

Stephen, Julia Duckworth. 1980. *Notes from Sick Rooms*. Introduction by Constance Hunting. Orono, Maine: Puckerbrush Press. Reprint of London ed. of 1883.

————. 1987. *Stories for Children, Essays for Adults: The Unpublished Writings of Julia Stephen*. Edited by Diane Gillespie and Elizabeth Steele. Syracuse: Syracuse University Press.

Stephen, Leslie. 1977. *Sir Leslie Stephen's Mausoleum Book*. Edited by A. Bell. Oxford: Oxford University Press.

Trombley, Stephen. 1981. *"All that Summer She Was Mad:" Virginia Woolf and Her Doctors*. London: Junction Books.

Walker, Nancy. 1988. Public presence and private self in Dickinson, James, and Woolf. In *The Private Self: Theory and Practice of Women's Autobiographical Writings*, edited by Shari Benstock, 272-303. Chapel Hill: University of North Carolina Press.

Wolfenstein, Martha. 1966. How is mourning possible? *Psychoanal. Study of the Child* 21:93-123.

————. 1969. Loss, rage, and repetition. *Psychoanal. Study of the Child* 24:432-60.

Woolf, Leonard. 1963. *Beginning Again: An Autobiography of the Years 1911 to 1918*. New York: Harcourt Brace Jovanovich.

————. 1967. *Downhill All the Way: An Autobiography of the Years 1919 to 1939*. New York: Harcourt, Brace and World.

————. 1969. *The Journey Not the Arrival Matters: An Autobiography of the Years 1939–1969*. New York: Harcourt, Brace and World.

————, and James Strachey, eds. 1969. *Letters: Virginia Woolf and Lytton Strachey*. London: Hogarth Press.

Woolf, Virginia. 1915 *The Voyage Out*. London: Penguin, 1992.

————. 1922. *Jacob's Room*. In *Jacob's Room and The Waves*. New York: Harcourt, Brace and World, 1959.

————. 1925. *Mrs. Dalloway*. New York: Harcourt, Brace and World, 1953.

————. 1925. *The Common Reader*. New York: Harcourt, Brace and World, 1953.

————. 1927. *To the Lighthouse*. New York: Harcourt, Brace.

————. 1929. *A Room of One's Own*. New York: Harcourt, Brace and World, 1957.

————. 1931. *The Waves*. In *Jacob's Room and The Waves*. New York: Harcourt, Brace and World, 1959.

————. 1932. Leslie Stephen. In *The Captain's Death Bed and Other Essays*. New York: Harcourt Brace Jovanovich, 1978.

————. 1942. Professions for Women. In *The Death of the Moth and Other Essays*. New York: Harcourt Brace Jovanovich, 1970.

————. (1975–80). *The Letters of Virginia Woolf*. Vols. 1–6. Edited by Nigel Nicolson and Joanne Trautman. London: Hogarth Press.

————. (1977–84). *The Diaries of Virginia Woolf*. Vols. 1–5. Edited by Anne Olivier Bell. New York: Harcourt Brace Jovanovich.

————. 1979. "Friendships Gallery." Edited by Ellen Hawkes. *Twentieth Century Literature* 25:270–302.

————. 1982. *Melymbrosia: An Early Version of The Voyage Out*. Edited by Louise DeSalvo. New York: New York Public Library.

————. 1985. *The Complete Shorter Fiction of Virginia Woolf*. 2d ed. Edited by Susan Dick. New York and London: Harcourt Brace Jovanovich.

————. 1986. *Moments of Being*. 2d ed. Edited by Jeanne Schulkind. New York: Harcourt Brace Jovanovich.

————. (1986–94). *The Essays of Virginia Woolf*. Edited by Andrew McNeillie. London: Hogarth Press.

————. 1990. *A Passionate Apprentice: The Early Journals of Virginia Woolf*. Edited by Mitchell A. Leaska. New York: Harcourt Brace Jovanovich.

Zwerdling, Alex. 1986. *Virginia Woolf and the Real World*. Berkeley: University of California Press.

Special Collections:

The Henry W. and Albert Berg Collection at the New York Public Library.

Department of Manuscripts, British Library.

Index

3 1170 00583 0314

Glenview Public Library
1930 Glenview Road
Glenview, Illinois